BORDER ZONE

John Agard was born in Guyana and came to Britain in 1977. His many books include nine collections from Bloodaxe, *From the Devil's Pulpit* (1997), *Weblines* (2000), *We Brits* (2006), *Alternative Anthem: Selected Poems* (2009), *Clever Backbone* (2009), *Travel Light Travel Dark* (2013), *Playing the Ghost of Maimonides* (2016), *The Coming of the Little Green Man* (2018) and *Border Zone* (2022). He publishes three books in 2022, the other two being *Inspector Dreadlock & Other Stories* (Small Axes) and a collection of children's poetry, *Follow that Word* (Hachette). He was awarded the Queen's Gold Medal for Poetry 2012, and in 2021 became the first poet to win BookTrust's Lifetime Achievement Award.

He won the Casa de las Américas Prize in 1982 for *Man to Pan*, a Paul Hamlyn Award in 1997, and a Cholmondeley Award in 2004. *We Brits* was shortlisted for the 2007 Decibel Writer of the Year Award, and he has won the Guyana Prize twice, first for *From the Devil's Pulpit* and then for *Weblines*. *The Coming of the Little Green Man* was a Poetry Book Society Special Commendation.

As a touring speaker with the Commonwealth Institute, he visited nearly 2000 schools promoting Caribbean culture and poetry. In 1993 he became the first Writer in Residence at London's South Bank Centre; in 1998 he was writer-in-residence for the BBC with the Windrush project; and in 2007 was writer in residence at the National Maritime Museum in Greenwich.

He is a popular children's writer whose titles include *Get Back Pimple* (Viking), *Laughter is an Egg* (Puffin), *Grandfather's Old Bruk-a-down Car* (Red Fox), *I Din Do Nuttin* (Red Fox), *Points of View with Professor Peekaboo* (Bodley Head) and *We Animals Would Like a Word with You* (Bodley Head), which won a Smarties Award. *Einstein, The Girl Who Hated Maths*, a collection inspired by mathematics, and *Hello H₂O*, a collection inspired by science, were published by Hodder Children's Books and illustrated by Satoshi Kitamura. Frances Lincoln Children's Books published his recent titles *The Young Inferno* (2008), his retelling of Dante, also illustrated by Satoshi Kitamura, which won the CLPE Poetry Award 2009, and *Goldilocks on CCTV* (2011). His first non-fiction work, *Book* (Walker Books, 2016), telling the history of books in the voice of the Book itself, was longlisted for the 2016 Carnegie Medal. In 2016 John Agard was presented with the 50th Eleanor Farjeon Award for his exceptional contribution to children's books.

He lives with the poet Grace Nichols in Sussex; they received the CLPE Poetry Award 2003 for their children's anthology *Under the Moon and Over the Sea* (Walker Books).

JOHN AGARD

Border Zone

BLOODAXE BOOKS

ISBN: 978 1 78037 588 5

First published 2022 by
Bloodaxe Books Ltd,
Eastburn,
South Park,
Hexham,
Northumberland NE46 1BS.

www.bloodaxebooks.com
For further information about Bloodaxe titles
please visit our website and join our mailing list
or write to the above address for a catalogue.

Supported using public funding by
ARTS COUNCIL
ENGLAND

Printed in Great Britain by Bell & Bain Limited, Glasgow, Scotland, on
acid-free paper sourced from mills with FSC chain of custody certification.

ACKNOWLEDGEMENTS

'Windrush Postscript' first appeared in the *Financial Times* *magazine* section featuring an article by William Wallis. 'Bards at the Crease' first appeared in *Griffith Review* (Australia).

Among the random sources I've dipped into for background to *Casanova the Philosopher*, I'd like to credit the following: *Casanova, Or, The Art of Happiness* by Lydia Clem (Allen Lane/ The Penguin Press, 1998); *Casanova* by Ian Kelly (Hodder & Stoughton, 2008); *Casanova* by John Masters (Michael Joseph, 1969); and of course *The Story of My Life* by the man himself, Giacomo Casanova (Penguin Classics, 2001).

Thanks to Millie Dobres for her filmic creative vision and collaboration on two short film poems, *Lewes to London Post-Lockdown* and *Wall Speaks*. The first was premiered at Depot cinema in Lewes during Black History Month 2021, thanks to the support of Carmen Slijpen, director of Depot. Both were presented together as *Poetry in Black and White* at the Lewes All Saints Centre for an event organised by Lewes Live Literature, thanks to director Mark Hewitt, who also presented a selection of his own short film collaborations with digital artist Matt Parsons.

Thanks to Satoshi Kitamura for yet another wonderfully arresting cover illustration. And thanks to Neil Astley, editor of Bloodaxe Books, for his patience, care and canny eye.

CONTENTS

LOVE IN A SCEPTRED ISLE

1

To see all that smoke rising from the chimneys
of London houses he'd first mistaken for factories
was really something for Victor to write home about
(with a postwar photo enclosed to prove it fact).
But from these same houses a sign said boldly
NO DOGS. NO GYPSIES. NO IRISH. NO BLACKS.
Here comes that thin line between survival and tact

2

and that suitcase (West Indians like to call their grip)
will with the years grow wrinkles in some attic,
that grip bearing witness to history's excess weight,
that grip packed with memory, dreams, hopes, faith
(and a bottle of rum and pepper sauce of course)
that humble grip containing hemispheres,
that talisman with winds of change to declare

3

surveying the scene from under an iconic trilby
like those *Windrush* ones who'd docked at Tilbury,
see him fresh-footing past red brick that looks alike
and the net curtains that cloister a window's eye
doubly useful for keeping the outside outside,
and for snatching sneak preview of an exotic newcomer.
Now Victor finds his walk slowly growing brisker

4

one winter, one winter, that's how long they'll last,
said then colonial secretary, Mr Creech-Jones,
placing his political faith in a sub-zero blast.
Trusting the English weather to dampen what hopes
they might have of growing into permanent Brits.
Only a matter of time before those gale force winds
make those sunshine foreigners settle for in-transit

5

a ticket-clipper for (we're getting there) British Rail?
A sunny postie loyal to a bag of Royal Mail?
Such options won't spring-up the step of Victor's day.
No, he sees himself more as a Caribbean Man Ray.
To his camera he would lend calypso's slanting eye.
Photography, you see, had long been his burning passion.
His break would come with a magazine called *Ethnic Fashion*

6

of course the white editor took some convincing
that the whole world being ethnic (strictly speaking)
what if Victor zoomed in, not just on so-called minorities,
but also turned his lens on the English ethnic majority?
Say close-ups of Morris dancers in bell-ribboned tunics?
What better way to embrace the English into the ethnic?
Victor feels like an anthropologist with each click

7

all the while graffiti crying in red from grey stone,
reminding him there's no black in the Union Jack!
Come to think of it, there's no sign of green either,
though green should please a North Sea islander.
See Victor aiming his lens at the spray-gunned reminder
of mindless rants on rundown walls. A familiar sight.
But what if the heart's walls were inscribed *Keep Britain White?*

8

Victor's first Christmas wasn't easy, that's for sure.
People listening to the Queen's message behind closed doors.
He missing that West Indian mummer-man in flouncy dress
masquerading on stilts to the beat of drum and fife,
bringing to Bethlehem a certain, shall we say, Creoleness.
And his grandmudda's black cake so well rum-spiced
a small boy feels merry as a kite from too many a slice

9

yet even amidst this blanket of Yuletide whiteness,
Victor is grateful for the smallest of epiphanies.
Like that Robin Red Breast, a feathered little Magus
gracing the doorstep with news of no them, no us.
An honour to meet this Christmas card celebrity,
who turns out to be a blood-bearing messenger
come to fill with light the stockings of dark December

10

back on a beach washed in Caribbean's blue aura,
his small-boy hands conjure sand into crumbling castles
of childhood's uncontrived architecture.
Now he's thinking the moment has come to have a go
at erecting his first snowman – a monument fleshed in snow.
Unlike those grand bronze affairs designed to impress,
his monument rejoices in simply melting into itself

11

all the while his ears getting used to *sorry... oh so sorry...*
these daily mantric permutations of apology.
Whether your leanings be Labour, Liberal, Tory,
the foreign ear best tune itself to the key of sorry.
Should you bump into a stranger, or for that matter,
should a stranger bump into you – get in there first.
Get in with your *oh so sorry* even when you feel to curse

12

now why does beware of the dog arrest his attention?
Back in his born-island the dogs were conditioned
to harass even the heels of a push-bike straggler.
Dog-kissing may be the done thing among dog-loving Brits,
but kissing a rottweiler is not on Victor's to-do list.
To pet or not to pet, that is the question for one
who views canines with trans-Altlantic circumspection

13

in his best cursive as mastered from a double-lined
exercise book drilled into his schoolboy's cranium,
Victor waxes lyrical on London via a postcard
(one with the pigeons grooming Lord Nelson's column).
Stamp lovingly licked. Destination back-a-yard.
O city of sirens wailing from a sea of wheels within wheels.
Like Kitchener once said, London is the place fo' me

14

and soon Victor finds himself singing fire's praises,
rejoicing in the smallest flame that blazes,
thankful as ever for that taken-for-granted miracle.
Imagine stepping out of a biting December wind
into a shiver-free abode, however humble
and your freezing-to-the-bone fingers rediscover
the Neolithic perk of that thing called paraffin heater

15

yes, a fire's glow has fast grown into an unsung friend,
a welcome rendezvous at a long winter day's end.
In times when central heating meant nouveau riche
and dinosaur heaters not yet state-of-the-art kitsch,
O those old radiators bringing instant incandescence,
ideal for warming hands (not to mention damp socks)
as the powers-that-be punctually turn back the clocks

16

no, not the fire of Judgement Day brimstone
his grandmudda would back up with the Good Book
watching from veranda her hibiscus flame of hope.
Not the fire of the unheard rioting in the streets.
Not the friendly fire fighting with itself in a war zone.
No, just the fire that's there to warm a hand.
The small spark that ignites the yes of man and woman

17

'is going yuh going England?' his grandmudda had said.
'Yuh navel-string, remember boy, not buried in snow...'
and with Victor's grip packed for overseas (the big O)
her gone-blind eyes needed no extra source of light
to pierce the geography of a grandson's voice.
And green as he was to the coming of the four seasons,
her trembling dry-leaf hand would be his first gift of autumn

18

and to this day Victor cherishes her amber ring,
his finger feeling spirit-blessed by her Leo eye
that watches over his footsteps winter to spring,
forever wrapping him in the sap of memories.
Still his guide from across an abyss of airmail blue,
even now as he washes his hands – an habitual
act, so ordinary, yet so charged with ritual

19

ah those airmail *(par avion)* letter forms –
red, blue, white, breathing hibiscus, sky, sea, foam.
Nostalgia's ingredients of a born-island home.
Now, with his star hitched to London's horizons,
he must acclimatise his ways to the four seasons
that can congregate in a single English day.
Yet in his inner ear palm trees still have their say

20

for those buried moments that return to you by post
nothing beats a grandmother's handwritten touch –
a spidery unfolding of feelings too delicate to be couched
in faceless typeface of marching regimented rows
that reveal no ripple of blood-throbbing ebbs and flows.
No picturing a trembling hand over a thin blue sheet
of paper where rivers of sentiments once more meet

21

leaving room for undotted i's and uncrossed t's,
keeping him in the loop with back-a-yard odysseys,
unsung but no less real, a letter brings a flutter
to the start of his day, a frisson to his first cuppa.
Praise be this envelope. Well-licked crosser of borders.
When homespun tidings come through the flap in the door,
his away-heart basks in the lamp light of a word

22

but pouring white rum in the four corners of his bedsit
(for the ancestors' sake) certainly won't go amiss.
No reason for changing that ingrained Creole habit.
So what if the floor has a freshly laid carpet?
You never know what imperial ghosts lurk under it.
Their views as regards foreigners in residence?
A libation may yet invoke peaceful co-existence

23

heaven shield thee England in thy ancient cause
from tyrant governments and ancient laws...
lines return from childhood rote of sweet John Clare
whose heartfelt rant knew no political correctness
to conscience-jolt those riding on the dispossessed.
Like those plantation owners who for crown and coffers
had built their dominions over dusky others

24

yet in the sun-hot of his small days, Victor was yet to see
Clare's dove in a mossy oak or hear the 'merry minstrelsy'
of the too long absent cuckoo. No, Victor's soundscape
was more a fanfare of parrots in the turret of a palm tree.
Or a toucan's gutturals somewhere among the seagrape.
All those English pastorals learnt for a schoolboy's test
had not prepared his stride for this inner city quest

25

and now by the waters of the Thames he sits down
but does not weep or resurrect the name of Babylon.
Yet there by the sweet waters of the tainted Thames,
he sees again those souls ships had robbed of names.
And though summer's light made light of Atlantic's baggage,
there he sits dreaming of Blake's New Jerusalem
coming of age. Redemption's revisioned anthem

26

and what if those sandalled feet that in ancient time
had walked upon England's mountains green
should return this time more trendily shod
(perhaps even surfing the net on an iPad)
mingling countenance divine with the nine-to-five,
singing of diversity in some foreign tongue
until the bells of green and pleasant minds are rung?

27

time for him to revive the old black suit and tie
to send-off a fellow West Indian pilgrim
under the monkish mantle of a South London sky.
No palm tree, no blue sea, to witness an innings' end.
Yet trees he still can't name (whether oak, birch, elm)
pay last respects. And of course, no shortage of rum
to sanctify the trek from the cold crematorium.

28

no season is ever a good season for dying.
Those on-time daffodils ringing the bells of spring
won't cushion the blow or leave a heart less bruised.
And all the honey summer's sun pours down
won't smooth a cheek furrowed by heartrending news.
Autumn's fluttering gold won't restore the grimly reaped
or winter's white confetti make a wedding of that final sleep

29

abide with me abide with me still sounding in his ears,
he returns to the four walls of his castle-bedsit
to face the whirlwind of thoughts mortality bears.
Not quite at home with the hyphenated Afro-Caribbean,
he hanging on to the beacon of his calypso habit,
leaving the tight-lipped jibes to stand outside his door.
Nothing the beat of a Sparrow or Kitchener can't cure

30

looks like daffy-down-dilly has come to town
in a yellow petticoat and a pretty green gown…
As a colonial boy, he'd memorised Wordsworth's paean
to daffodils but now he meets one of those golden
hosts winking St David bright from a Welshman's chest.
Oh, if old Wordsworth was around, he'd be impressed
to hear a black man calling windy March blessed

31

there's a brown girl in de ring tralalala
and she looks like a sugar inna plum…
ah, how well he remembers that small-days game
when sunny back-a-yard was his run-free kingdom.
Show me yuh motion…skip across de ocean…tralalala…
yes, he's lived to see 1970s Britain bopping to Boney M
an ocean away from a tropical schoolyard anthem

32

amazed as ever at how a slice of sunshine
can help bliss-up the contours of the British face.
Gents, trousers rolled to kneecap, eyes divinely closed.
Ladies, chilled-out in parks, browning more than toes.
'Hot enough for you?' is how strangers address him.
Sometimes he has a mind to play the Devil's Advocate
and reply, 'too hot for me, I prefer the winter mate'

33

'tell you what, mate,' says the black cab driver in full flow.
'tell you what gets me 'bout this flipping country,
a couple of weeks' good sunshine, and guess what?
Hose-pipe bans, no paddling pools, the bleeding lot.
They're taking our money for water bills and all that,
but they 'aven't a clue, not a bloody clue 'ave they, bruv?'
Which foreigner dare doubt a man who has the Knowledge?

34

keeping a low profile but not quite as low as limbo,
under the sudden benediction of a summer shower,
a far cry from a humming bird's epiphany,
today he will rejoice in the common good of rain,
that generous gesture of the sky's democracy.
Now a roof of slate greets that grey crescendo
making his dreamtime head both bridge and pillow

35

to tell the truth, he thinks he could get by without
the kiss of life from a coconut's jellied pout
direct from the vendor's bottle-lamp pushcart,
or without the rain's flamenco on zinc sheet roof.
But when London hurries itself into rush-hour dark,
there's one simple thing he misses more than ever –
the fireflies lighting themselves at evening's altar

36

reaching for sugarcane's hand in Shepherd's Bush Market –
a clear case of transatlantic long-time-no-see, mate.
Like listening to the water inside a jet-lagged coconut
and hearing an ancient ocean-salted saga. Back to roots.
But now that plump crystal ball of a green breadfruit
so out-of-the-blue it seems downright oracular.
Enough for Victor to explode into the vernacular

37

turning now to say a lil hello to Avocado
which the Aztecs call *ahuacatl* (translated simply
as testicle… Achilles' heel to a cricket ball's trajectory).
Old folks say when avocados reveal their green bollocks,
it's time for gentlemen to start taking stock.
Smiling to himself, he thinks of a question for the lads?
What if your family jewels were diced into salads?

38

among this diaspora of blushing mangoes, guavas,
bananas, papayas, pineapples in their unpeeled orbit,
Brussels sprouts hobnobbing with chili, okra, cassava,
what can he hope for next? Perhaps blue pomegranates?
Blue ones with apple crumble might be nice, he reflects.
Or do blue pomegranates grow only on rabbis' gowns
to shade the seeds of scattered generations?

39

knock-knock-who dat? His answer? *Two Enochs.* A name
that rings a bell from Genesis to Wolverhampton,
First Enoch (great grandfather of Noah) seated in God's glory.
Then came that other Enoch, seated front bench Tory.
One Enoch aflame with heaven's star-filled mandala.
One Enoch foaming at immigration. A classical scholar.
Long before the iconic rise of chicken tikka masala

40

whoever said in every life a little rain must fall
wasn't thinking of test match confrontation
when hopes hinge on wield of bat and swing of ball
and Empire's children equate cricket with liberation.
Whether sky spitting or pissing down (as locals say),
please God, hold back your saliva and your pee.
Not now. Not when West Indies sniffing victory

41

for the touch-starved, where better to hug up humanity
than when carnival rolls out its carnal tapestry
at Notting Hill Gate in hopefully-hot August
and monumental Europe lets down its spinal column.
If only for a day, forgetting the tribal them and us.
Come bank holiday, the Gate is the place to go.
Yeah man, the gateway to where flesh turns rainbow

42

but how sum up summer's dance on a branch of skin
when the sun goes round its own mulberry bush?
The kind of day for a rum and ginger with loud ice
as far away as possible from the madding crush.
Not necessarily on a bingeing far-off package tour,
but somewhere O much much nearer home –
that place where singing flesh meets singing bone

43

what if the native ladies beckon hidden promise,
well-met by midsummer's metamorphosis
when a much sought-after top-to-bottom tan
recasts in bronze the Anglo-Saxon epidermis?
And though lust knows no bound of creed or clan,
would it be unwise to provoke the tribal boot
for a fleeting frisson of forbidden fruit?

44

yet heart and heart can click where you least expect.
And there in a bookshop selling remaindered stock,
behind the till sits one with a smile he'd call bounty-full.
'After something special?' she asks. 'Or just browsing?'
Sweet Jesus, he thinks, get a grip, she's just being helpful.
But something about her is making music in his head.
So he browses much longer than he'd intended

45

coincidence? Fate? Chance? Luck? Call it what you will.
But who should he meet but that haunting figure
made flesh again emerging from Lavender Hill,
just back from a yoga class and still in her leggings.
And when she says, 'I live down the road in Battersea,
what you up to? Fancy popping in for a quick cuppa?'
he gets the feeling cloud nine had rained down manna

46

then God forbid, as Lady Ill-luck would have it,
she keeps a dog that leaps to nuzzle Victor's orbit.
'Got bitten once as a child,' he's compelled to admit.
'He won't harm you,' she says. 'A real softie.
From Battersea Dog's Home. I call him Cerberus.'
'You mean after Cerberus as in Homer's three-head
monster guarding the gateway to the dead?

47

'I see you're well brushed up on your mythology,'
she says. 'What would I do without Cerberus for company?'
Of course, Victor doesn't confess to his canine precaution.
When she informs him the said Cerberus is Dachshund,
his mind thinks *Achtung* from those war comics of his teens.
But not wanting to go down in the lady's estimation,
he strokes the beast's head with inward trepidation

48

now across the expanse of a white tablecloth lake
the poised teapot extends its swan-sleek bill
leaving not one telltale concentric ripple.
And though tea was not his favourite tipple,
his native taste buds are getting used to their fill
of Earl Grey and scones with their strawberry grin.
Learning from a sugar cube, a way of blending in

49

and though the canefields resurrect their embers
even from the golden crystal in a teacup,
there's something in the air beyond decorum.
Something about the way this heaven-sent stranger
pours herself into her delicate Wedgwood blue
has him thinking he could become a sucker for a brew.
Or should that be Atlantic's reviving residue?

50

can one be of Caribbean stock and not be breezy?
Must he prove himself a sunshine-and-rhythm prodigy?
Breathing flesh and blood into that stereotype?
Living up to the snapshot of limbo laidback hype?
No, on this occasion, he'll be vulnerable Victor,
exercising his human right to be a little awkward.
His two tropical left feet as clumsy as his heart

51

what if she was a far cry from those wenches of fiction?
As in, for example, the milkmaid, yes, the buxom one,
ruddy not only in her cheeks but in her misdemeanour.
Well, the grass on the other side, they say, seems greener.
Wasn't Chaucer's Bath-bred dame a merry wanton?
Or are such figments found only in the flesh of the Canon?
Yet how his mouth would grow to savour the name: Rhiannon

52

something in the rhythm of her voice (not quite English)
suddenly strikes him like a syncopated jazz riff.
She says her roots were the colourful side of Cardiff
(her way of signalling Tiger Bay's dockland area)
where a choir of Welsh miners once lifted their spirits
hallelujah-high on Paul Robeson's *Ole Man River*.
Already purity had begun to unfasten its fetters.

53

as for his accent, Rhiannon says, 'Wait. Let me guess.
You don't sound anything like Lenny Henry,
so you're definitely not from the Black Country...'
She could aways recognise that Caribbean rhythm,
but where place him on the linguistic continuum?
Victor's mix-and-match away-swing vocal delivery
wasn't what C.L.R. James had meant by *Beyond a Boundary*

54

when Rhiannon tells him she'd recently gone veggie,
he thinks there goes jerk chicken and goat curry.
But no point letting the matter of dietary intake
get in the way of strangers growing into soul-mates.
Yet, even for the sake of Cupid's unprejudiced arrow,
he'd draw the line at quiche with roasted marrow.
Not while a leg of lamb still makes a dull Sunday glow

55

one day she promises that she'll do him
her Rhiannon version of Jamaican pot roast.
(minus the dreaded leg of beef, of course).
A recipe from that TV chef whose name she forgot.
Victor in turn promises her a curry (minus the goat).
He swears there'll be no trace of a cloven hoof
if ever she should come to dine under his roof

56

'like your amber,' she says, touching his ring.
'A sunshine stone,' she adds. 'Wards off evil,
and points, so they say, to new beginnings.'
'My grandmudda,' he says, 'believes in such things
that you might call beyond the ken of humankind.
In her nineties and still kicking, though now blind.
As for her marbles, as sharp as amber's eye...'

57

relating how he'd come to be, not a mother's boy,
but what you might call a grandmudda's protege,
sadness wells up to his throat as he tells of that day,
that ill-fated day – Good Friday of all days,
when his parents had set off on a ferry excursion,
leaving his toddling self in his grandmudda' care,
brushing aside the old lady's word: beware

58

for his mum and dad had put it down to superstition,
the needless worry passed on by an old wives' tale –
that to travel on Jesus' death-day is to tempt doom.
Same as raising a kite on that day of Crucifixion
is to invite (as old folks say) a tragedy waiting to happen.
That ferry, sad to tell, went down without resurrection.
His grandmudda all toddling Victor had for his lean-upon

59

and Rhiannon, hearing of Victor's tribulation
at so early an age, lets instinct win over caution.
She clasps this stranger's hand in a one-to-one –
the silent dialogue of hand nesting in hand.
And if curiosity should stoke the fire under the skin,
then blame it all on a midsummer's kindling.
'You do your grandmother proud,' she says, smiling

60

and see Victor now on this green-fingered patio
(where pots, tubs, hanging baskets, put forth their blooms –
all manner of herbs of which he hadn't a clue)
and see Rhiannon guiding him to rosemary, tarragon, rue,
not to mention that futuristic visit to Kew Gardens
where she'd introduce him to migrant cedars from Lebanon,
making him recall how Sheba had laid with Solomon

61

his gardening nous, practically speaking, next to nil.
Not even a window-box graces his window-sill.
Though new to mulching, dead-heading, ground cover,
he knew this much – there's more to it than a green finger.
From a world where gardener once doubled as executioner,
those pink tulips, now at ease with being suburban,
still contain within themselves an Ottoman's turban

62

and that vase of dahlias dazzling a dining table
in those hollow stems lie a hidden parable.
Acocoxochitl in the tongue of feathered Montezuma,
now for sale at B & Q – a perennial tuber.
Dahlia, thriving in the name of Dahl, that Swedish apostle
of Linnaeus, the classifier of plants by genus.
Even the ones already named by the indigenous

63

and what's to learn from common garden peas
(more than happy to run beside runner beans?)
Perhaps this. That hybrids are the mother of variety –
producing offspring, they say, of good vigour and yield.
Though Victor is more of an armchair gardener,
he thinks garden peas have found a way to be liberated.
And he rather likes the sound of open-pollinated

64

then Rhiannon turns to him with an odd question:
'Mind if I ask if you believe in reincarnation?
But don't you get the feeling we've done this before?'
Trusting there's no catch in her query, he replies,
'Strange, but I too feel I've crossed this very threshold.'
Thinking to himself, if this moment be paradise restored,
then let the heavenly hosts cry encore, and again, encore

what more will she reveal from up her sleeveless sleeve?
She tells him she'd been back to browsing her Kabbalah
that urges every exiled Adam to seek his inner Eve?
What's God without his female half, divine Shekhinah?
Meanwhile, his daydreams drift to the blooming buddleia.
And not wanting to stray too far from his comfort zone,
Victor sighs, 'I guess it all comes back to flesh and bone'

66

'mind if I stroke that belly?' he adds (with a hint of mischief)
directing Rhiannon's gaze to the pot-bellied midriff
of the Laughing Buddha squatting boldly on her patio.
'At your own risk,' she says, her eyes all laughter's glow.
Like that secret which had exploded the Buddha into hysterics.
Like his grandmudda's belly-warming eruptions into stitches
when evening's fireflies were her flickering accomplices

67

'another cuppa?' she winks, but doesn't real need to,
for the fledgling in his loins had begun to tweeter.
All the signals pointing to an unlegislated meeting
between contrary heart and contrary heart.
For how partition the blood's unruly stirring
between the ones on whom the snow has left its mark
and the ones whose birthright is the sun's direct dart?

68

with these two finding each other's otherness inspiring,
and with chemistry's blaze well and truly spiralling,
one thing, as they say, would lead to the next.
The ice of no dissolving into a fountain of yes.
Abandon joining flanks with the arrows of desiring.
And though the mind musters all its defences,
two castles formed of flesh crumble to a sweet caress

69

trust that Bard of Avon, known for bawdy wisecracks,
to come up with playing the beast with two backs.
The Bard, of course, didn't specify the location,
whether al fresco or plushly-bottomed on a cushion.
It was up to the two individuals, Victor presumed,
whether they choose to disrobe in the bedroom
or unravel on a sofa under a throw of red white and blue

70

and from the perch of themselves they'd hoist their flight
to a place where history's cracks let in love's light,
finding a way to circumnavigate those borders
that colour the connecting of horizon with horizon.
And merging their separate zones into soul-mates one,
their fingers, his and hers, like two cuddling crabs
scuttle beyond the parametres of race and flag

71

to these two castaways on the island of a single pillow,
that sound of a breeze imitating a murmur
is only the breathing of lover to new-found lover,
the whisper of sweet nothings in the ear's archipelago.
Was it like this in Eden's grove before that fall?
This ebbing and flowing of other into otherness,
mimicing the timeless tide dissolving into itself

72

under the voyeur eye of that dachshund, Cerberus,
(a four-legged Cupid at the foot of the duvet)
their frolics would make a rhapsody of a rumpus,
as besotted adults do when they revert to rude play.
But Victor's thoughts flash to Napoleon's wedding night,
when Bonaparte got bitten by his Josephine's pet mutt,
luckily on his ankle (but it could have been his butt)

73

of course, Victor is the kind who counts his blessings,
relieved that Cerberus keeps to the foot of the bed.
Things could have been much worse, it must be said,
had Rhiannon called her dachshund after Damocles.
Imagine, a little doggie sword dangling over his head!
His grandmudda had taught him blessings come disguised.
So Victor now abides the canine as third-party ally

74

but as the buddleia puts forth its butterfly bloom
for every branch to greet an ambassador that flutters,
and as the frisky lambs turn a meadow to a boudoir,
and as the bees caress a petal in the honeyed hour,
likewise did our two lovebirds feed upon each other,
and who could blame them for overlooking one truth? –
Such doing can lead to offspring – in short, foetal fruit

75

no, neither had given thought to being a dad or a mum.
Lost in the now, simply taking each day as it comes.
Not dwelling on the nuts and bolts of parental pros and cons.
For though Rhiannon had been attuned to her lunar clock,
by the time the embryonic penny had dropped,
mother nature's telltale bump would be well on the rise –
a crescent moon turning her tummy to a skyline

76

having lost both his parents, while still a toddler
(ever thankful to that angel of a grandmudda)
Victor greets Rhiannon's news as tidings of great joy.
Maybe a little Victor? A bouncing baby boy?
Then again, he reminds himself, a bouncing baby girl
would be just as bountiful – a bundle-full harvest.
And with his head on Rhiannon's belly, he feels blessed

77

and thanks to the technology of ultrasound,
he gets his first-time view of a womb in throbbing bud,
while Rhiannon basks in the miracle of her own bloom.
Her inner self now moulded into a fluttering fruit,
making of two human spheres one hemisphere.
Victor gazes at the scan, his eyes gobsmacked captive.
If only his negatives were half as pulsing positive

78

but there was another trump up mother nature's sleeve,
when from the shifting fog of the sonographer's screen,
appear two mini-astronauts caught in inner space.
Or looked at another way, two spiralling little dolphins.
Or to put it plainly, Rhiannon hears she's expecting twins.
'Babies are like the buses,' she laughs. 'Don't you agree?
You hope for one, then they come in twos, even threes'

79

the twin girls (if you must know) were named Deva and Diva.
Names that may sound somewhat devilish on first-hearing,
yet mystically and sonically speaking, most endearing.
Deva's smile would light up the house, Diva born for an aria.
Wasn't their dad named Victor after that Queen Victoria
(courtesy of British rule) and their mum, Rhiannon,
after that horse-riding immortal of the *Mabinogion*?

80

Victor prays these girls walk good in hybrid roots,
for he has seen generation follow generation
born of Empire's deeds coming home to roost.
Beyond the swagger in their stride and tongue,
may the globe shine its light upon their vision.
And beyond the easy glamour of tough-talk cred,
may forward dreaming make a planet of their head

82

meanwhile in post-Brexit Britain outside Marks & Sparks
a busking band is brassing out *Amazing Grace*
(that hymn from a reformed Newton, a clergyman,
who had once captained a vessel of the vilest trade).
The buskers, Victor soon learns, are Eastern European.
Now the trumpet revives that 70s anthem *I Will Survive*
and for a moment no one looks afraid or petrified

83

take our country back becoming the tribal mantra
among those who'd rather the curve of their banana
not be dictated to by the law-makers of Brussels
across that intermediary Styx known as the Channel
that made Napoleon have more than second thoughts.
O Happy Day, chorus as one the Brexiteer zealots,
while EU disciples cry forgive them for they know not...

84

and in his twilight years Victor will sing of autumn
(his favourite season, even more than spring)
for that's when green leaf turns golden brown earring
and he'll be stepping through nature's fallen treasure.
When love's radiance beckons strides to the future,
he doesn't plan on chaining himself to a crippling rage.
Learning from the autumn trees to let go of baggage

85

for he has no intention of migrating in reverse.
Back to his navel-strings (courtesy of the grim hearse)
for a prodigal son's sunny send-off six feet under.
Not for him the band-yuh-belly-and-bawl graveside rites
No, he's here to stay on this mongrel sceptred isle.
No place he'd rather be than Kitchener's fair city –
London – O precious metropolis set in a plural sea

86

that remaindered bookshop where Victor and Rhiannon
had first met remaindered too. Like so many things. Gone.
Now a Nero or maybe a Costa (one can never be sure).
Where bounded spines once stood in upright repose
now the hub of have-in-have-out flat whites and cappuccinos.
And while the powers-that-be spread their gospel of spin,
two unsceptred hearts make room to let the other in

NAVIGATING CONTINENTS

Flag Speaks

1

I've come a long way
from ribbons
on spears
and garlands
of feathers
heading a fanfare
of tribal others.
Now nations march
to the grammar
of my squares
and rectangles
(not to mention
the odd triangle).
On grand parades
you'll see me displayed
to the height of my glory.
The centre of ritual attention.
But I stay calm and carry on
as any flag
worth its weight
in cloth would do

2

up a pole
down a pole
ever playing
my starring role
in the fabric
of a nation's unfolding
of what's known
as Independence.

How I have danced
in the neutral breeze
for monarchs overseas
and seen the colours
of myself reshuffled
for the long shackled
about to step
into their own stride

3

for I too have heard of that feeling
called national pride
from the well-informed lips
of the transatlantic winds
that keep me flapping
as well as up-to-date
on history's shifting weight,
those winds that bring me tidings
of risings and uprisings,
of timely severings
from a mother country's
absentee apron strings,
a people defined
by Empire's still visible spectre
rebirthing into their own mirror.
And so at midnight's chime
I become a banner
for a milestone beginning
hoisted skywards
as a fluttering monument
to the future.
And when freedom tolls
see how I lord it
up my stately pole
to trumpet and drum roll

And in the reckoning hour
when old rages grow mute
I command
a multitude's salute
and a speechless minute
falls across the land

4

oh what would
the United Nations
the Commonwealth
the Latin American Confederation
the Arab Emirates
(in short the globe)
do without the likes of me
and all my colourful kin?
We whose silent tongue
is flaunted in the wind.
Therefore unravel
what hidden meaning you will
from my flying
geometry of colours.

5

full-mast
I am an emblem
of protocol and celebration.
Half-mast
I am the drooping shroud
of mass lamentation.
To you who wave me
from the bonded crowd
what words can a flag offer
beyond the fervour
of slogans
that shadow my rainbow?

Yet since a flag also knows
how it feels to be thrown
to the fury of flames
(and I shall call no names)
on behalf of every flag
I ask of all who wave me to order:
am I the mere cloth you brandish
to a marching creed
basking in the vanquished?
Or am I a nation's handkerchief
flown from a flagstaff of justice?
As democratic as sun and moon.

Windrush Postscript

Call them *Windrush* pilgrims, pioneers,
or simply the followers of a leap of faith
when dreams were coloured red white and blue
and Tilbury Docks signalled hope renewed.

But Red rewinds the mind to forgotten colonies
that once bled for a sceptred isle overseas.
White points to the page that fiddled a continent.
Blue for the sky that surveys all without judgement.

These dressed-to-the-nines *Windrush* newcomers
were supposed to survive only one winter.
Seventy winters later, that *Windrush* word
returns to haunt Britain's tribal corridors.

Which leads one to ask by way of postscript:
have they forgotten the ship in citizenship?

A Citizen's Tale

In the West Country he kept his vowels rolled.
Did his best Walter Ralegh impression.
Keen to blend in with clotted cream and scones.
Yet always that foreign son of Devon.

So he headed hot-foot for the Sussex Downs,
Rambled past Albion's chalk. Poppies rippling.
Minded his hedgerow as he thumbed his Kipling.
Yet the locals took his arrival for asylum.

Next stop Yorkshire's wuthering moors.
Learnt to mingle his walk with Heathcliff's stride.
Drank bitter with cricket village-green-style.
Yet overheard that whispered word: exile.

So will this sceptred isle of Sunday roast
see itself as the forever imperial host
to feet that walked this land from ancient time
when black Romans once surveyed Saxon kind?

While Enoch Powell's lot wave their tribal banner,
the Brit nation salutes chicken tikka masala.
So with a citizen's taste for the proverbial cuppa,
he makes room for spicy grub and creamy afters.

Happy to be one us and one of them.
How else do we build a new Jerusalem?

Doing My Bit for Pomp and Pageantry

(for John Blanc, described as the Black Tudor, an equestrian trumpeter at the courts of Henry VII and Henry VIII. He is depicted among the King's entourage on the royal Westminster Tournament Roll.)

In Norman French the name has a ring that's nice.
Not John Blanke, John Blanc, to be precise.

Shall we say a Tudor gentleman of colour?
Or one who brought colour to the Tudor court?
What's in a name leaves ample room to ponder
for am I not John White the Black
and Black John White rolled into one turban?

In days when the Henrys ruled the royal roost
and the King himself took to the manly joust
I hailed the thrust of lance with trumpet blast.
I, the equestrian exotic of the retinue,
blowing for every pence of my shillings' due.

Thus the North African winds had followed me
to an England known both as Olde and Merry.
Yes, I whose Moorish skin echoed midnight's key,
surveyed from a turban's rainbow my adopted Albion.
And to those white cliffs my lips put forth their clarion.

Not quite a fanfare for diversity.
Simply doing my bit for pomp and pageantry.
Yet when history's footnotes begin to grow more bold
and the heart's tapestry unrolls its spectrum,
hear again my trumpet's dark riffs rising out of vellum.

Gents of the Gentry

Bragging on is just not on.
Bragging on is rather common.
One must hold one's tongue, mustn't one?

It's called being an upper class gent.
We like to keep our rages reticent.
We've been raised on understatement.

Self-hoo-haa is such bother. Crass.
Self-effacement, we say, shows class.
What's called aristocratic gravitas.

Yes, we leave bragging to the Yanks.
Who cares if they think us tight-lipped cranks?
To self-inflation we say no thanks.

So we keep a stiff-upper-lip veneer,
long as we remain your lords and peers.
Only fair, dear boy, only fair.

So here's to the old self-ridicule.
When combined with divide and rule,
it provides a jolly handy tool.

We are, you see, of the landed gentry.
And by virtue of our pedigree
we land on our feet ever so gently.

With the Accent on Accent

(For Tom Leonard (1944-2018) Glaswegian poet and man of integrity, known for highlighting accent as one way of usually telling the one in the dock from the one on the bench)

1

There was this judge of high station
who pronounced every sentence
in received pronunciation.
None could fault his plummy cadence
when he intoned incarceration.

2

In apple-picking Kent, this polyglot gent
took pride in being a man of many an accent.
All had stood him in good stead when tested
though once while rambling middle England
he found myself stopped, searched, arrested.
'Since my demeanour was sartorially legal,
and being neither armed nor indeed pissed,
I could only presume, with all due respect,
that my black lips flavoured with the Oxford lisp
must have have labelled this citizen suspect.'

3

An old sea dog, sea dog was he,
that West Country Sir Walter Ralegh.
Rolling his vowels most ardently,
he'd announce himself *Water Raw-ley.*

Said he one day to Queen Elizabeth,
'Mind that puddle, Your Highness.
I'll doff my coat to greet your footsteps.
And may the mud count itself blessed.'

'O Water, my Water,' replied Queen Lizzie.
'How I do thirst for your flattery.
You roll your vowels with such courtly glee,
you charm as well as make light my Crown.
Do talk to me dirty in broad Devon.'

4

There's this mate of mine of whom I'll now tell.
Born and bred within earshot of Bow Bells,
A Cockney-nurtured Eastender to the core.
Rhyming slang breathing through his every pore.
And there's me inching my way down the stairs
while he (bless him) would choose to navigate
the spiralling descent of apple and pears.
And dressed to the nines in three-piece suit,
he'd sigh, 'mate, don't I look too bloody cute
in de old pinstriped whistle and flute?'

5

There's this Black Brit from the Black Country,
(that is to say, the West Midlands.)
Grown used to being taken for a Brummie.
Often asked, 'So if you're from the Black Country,
have they got white people where you come from?'
That's when our Black Brit would do his posh impression:
'You've got me there, old chap. I'll ask my white mum.'

6

And out of the rippling archives of the Clyde
that still cradles the ghosts of Glasgow's past,
one homeless soul proclaimed to hurrying passers-by
who lent but half an ear to his glottal gravitas.

'It's dem what's born with a gold spoon up their ass
that shifts the goalposts for common folk. Upper class.
That poshy-spokey lot what think themselves superior,
though their cupboard hoards some slave-owning ancestor.

Meritocracy, my ass! More like inherit-ocracy!
The H-word comes to mind alright. Hypocrisy.
Nowt to do with moral fibre. What's that, brother?
Nowt to do with your vision for the future.

Who gives a toss 'bout your talent or sexual bent!
Sorry, pal, it's all to do with your bleeding accent!

The Discharge of the Un-light Brigade

(with apologies to Alfred Lord Tennyson's 'Charge of the Light Brigade')

Roast beef to right of them
Roast beef to left of them
Roast beef in front of them
    Their stomachs thundered
To Britannia's bell,
Boldly they dined and well
On empire's bounty.
How good to eat and swell
For King and country
  John Bull and company

Forward the Un-light Brigade
Heavy with fruits of trade
And every man there knew
   Some one had plundered:
Their's not to question why
Their's not to testify
Their's but to do and lie
For King and country
  John Bull and company

Flashed all their silver ware
Flashed all their molars bare
Savouring their gullets there
   Plunged in their clouds of smoke
Up to their nose in Port
Merchant and banker
And of profits they spoke
For King and country
  John Bull and company

Roast beef to right of them
Roast beef to left of them
Roast beef behind them
    Was there a man prepared
For when empires fade?
Not when tablecloths are laid
And stomachs thundered
Forward the Un-light Brigade!
    O heavy the discharge they made!

How Delroy Dee Lost His Job at English Heritage House

Welcome all to Huntingberry Hideaway –
A typical non-listed English country house.
I'm Delroy Dee, your tourist guide for the day.

Any questions, ladies and gentlemen, feel free
to stop me in the tracks of my full flow.
I'm at your service. And just call me DD.

Observe acres and acres of green splendour,
once the stamping ground of deer, fox, hare,
before the hounds heeded the lord of the manor

and at his horn prepared to bloody their fangs.
But even the upper-crust-dem need a hobby.
Let's not go into fox-hunting rights and wrongs.

Try to remember as you view the surroundings
you've come to enjoy an English country house.
We're not a museum of history's wrongdoings.

Lose yourself in the magnificent parkland.
Don't dwell too much on the mahogany door.
True enough, it was harvested by enslaved hands

in a dispossessed colony. Transatlantic legacy.
But you didn't hear me say the S-word, get my drift?
Ladies and gentlemen, step this way to luxury.

Dis carpet you're about to experience (tread light)
is plusher than plush Persian. But the windy-windy
staircase once stood upright under Jamaica sky.

Sadly, the forests of JA have been depleted.
But to be fair, without a touch of mahogany,
an English country house is never completed.

I must warn you the staircase steeper than it look.
And looks, as you well know, can be deceiving.
One American academic writing some kinda book

was so busy-busy taking notes and a selfie,
the fellow back-back till he back-back right over.
Thank God de carpet cushioned him in gentility.

So far so good. Like I said, you can fire question
to I-man whenever de mood come over you.
I'm all for a lil interactive interrogation.

All you who love God's creatures great and small,
check what a-go on over dat mantelpiece –
a tiger head, yes…un-live and direct from Bengal

(give thanks for de Egyptian art of taxidermy
because if dat tiger was up and running
we'd all end up as stuffing in a tiger belly).

Rewind to de Raj – Queen Victoria well enthroned –
and the owner of this house, Lord Huntingberry
dreaming of a little Taj Mahal to call his very own.

The Taj Mahal, as you know or might not know,
goes back to 1632 when the Mughal, Shah Jahan,
made his love for Mumtaz Mahal a public show.

So for his own wife, Lord Huntingberry had built
an ensuite dome-shaped replica here upstairs
(he named it the Mahal Taj to put right any guilt).

What the Huntingberrys got up to for diversion
is dem own kinky business – but how they raked
in their millions is not a million-dollar question.

That's for me to know and you folks to decipher.
Conscience have a way of zooming home to roost.
Hindus call it karma... fruit of the tree of empire...

Anyway, just for the record, dat oversized statue
of Lord Huntingberry cantering high in bronze...
if you would like my humble point of view...

I ain't saying pull it down and toss it to oblivion.
But if dat statue wasn't taking up so much space
you'd have a lot more room to let in de horizon.

Ladies and gentlemen, dat's Delroy Dee opinion.
Still no questions? Not an inkling of a query?
Very well. Forward to the Mahal Taj... no hurry...

Wall Speaks

I'm there to keep insiders in, outsiders out.
My silence speaks volumes on behalf of border
between nation and nation, other and other.

The dividing god line that says US–Mexico,
Iraq–Iran, Palestine–Israel, Austria–Slovenia,
China–North Korea, North Korea–South Korea…

But should I, Wall, carry on with this litany
that spells out the meaning of us and them?
And to which do I owe my loyalty?

I simply stay mute. Play my humble part.
Be the guard dog that does not wag or bark.
Uncomplaining. Just there. Standing my ground.

But the winds of history have taken their toll.
The centuries creep into my every crevice.
Even my barbed-wired head has seen better days.

For too long I've given stalwart service.
Been there to stop the barbarians in their tracks.
Now brick by crumbling brick, I await what next.

Diversity in de Market

(calypso poem)

(spoken)

To learn how dis ting diversity does operate
I went by Brixton market to investigate,
how de fruit and veg dem does integrate.
Ah saw Apple and Mango conversing cosily
Ripe Plantain had no quarrel with Broccoli.
Aubergine don't bear grudge 'gainst Piri-Piri.
I was impressed how Pineapple spoke sweetly
and when Red Pepper responded discreetly
I knew de fruit and veg dem could teach a nation
de secret of harmonious cohabitation.
So if you want learn 'bout dis ting diversity,
observe Butternut Squash and de little Lychee

(sung /calypso tempo)

> *In de fruit and veg market it was plain to see*
> *de red yellow purple green live in harmony.*
> *Yes, fruit and veg dem show each other respect,*
> *no, Cucumber never raise a finger to Courgette,*
> *no, Cucumber never raise a finger to Courgette*

(spoken)

Then I saw Saltfish chatting up Chorizo
like de two o' dem does talk de same lingo.
Gammon and Mackerel held no grievance.
Black Pudding and Salami struck up alliance.
So if you want learn 'bout social etiquette
just study de ways of Oxtail Veal Brisket

(sung/calypso tempo)

> *In de fish and meat market too it was plain to see*
> *de black white pink brown also live in harmony.*
> *Yes, fish and meat dem show each other respect,*
> *no, Ah never see a fight between two fillet yet,*
> *man, Ah never see a fight between two fillet yet.*

Potato Speaks

What I say is that, if a man really likes potatoes,
he must be a pretty decent sort of fellow.

A.A. MILNE

Call call me Spud, Tattie, Prattie, Fries, I'm not fussed.
In a womb of earth I lie, a curled-up foetus,
my flesh my gift whatever your colour or status.

And though I admit that a potato a day
may not, like Apple, keep the doctor away,
I stand here to say my piece come what may.

But before I, Potato, unpeel my point of view,
may I remind citizens of the red white and blue
of my abduction from my homeground Peru –

I your humble taken-for-granted tuber,
whom you douse in ketchup, salt, vinegar,
I who am both indigenous and foreigner,

now inseparable kin to your fish and chips,
I who fill with warmth the freezing famished.
Well adapted to British kitchen and kinship

I'll gladly bear the brunt of whatever sin
you lay at my wrinkled door. Like that famine,
the root of Ireland's flesh and blood uprooting.

But wasn't it your A.A. Milne (and I quote)
who said that any man who really likes potatoes
must be a pretty decent sort of fellow?

Sorry folks, no disrespect, I assure you,
to the creator of cuddly Winnie the Pooh
but I've known potato-lovers of fascist view.

Suckers for potatoes, fried, roasted, mashed, boiled,
yet from closeness to the Stranger they recoil,
preferring the Stranger to keep to elsewhere soil.

Meanwhile, I'll be there for you, ever at your side.
There, at home on your plate, I happily reside –
the edible prophet surveying all through blind eyes.

Biscuit Speaks

I may be part of the shortbread family
but that's no reason to shorten my name to *bikkie*.
I'm everything I've been cracked up to be.

Day in day out I'm nibbled, munched, scoffed,
whether by working-class or so-called toff.
Looks like my destiny is to live for my own ruin.

No one cares enough to even ask my origin.
But I'll have you know in the mouth of a Roman
I was *bis coctus*? (Twice cooked in translation.)

From *bis coctus* to *bikkie*! My God! What a comedown!
And as for my Arabic kin by the name of *Kaak*,
don't let's go there, mate, for I'll tell you what.

Cousin Kaak exudes rosewater and almond
with a tiara of (wait for it) toasted sesame seeds.
Alright for some, ain't it? It's called biscuit hierarchy!

People are under the illusion I'm just a snack.
But I'm discipline's ambassador wrapped in a pack.
I test your self-control. Try one of me and one only.

Got ya! Can't resist another, can ya? Meanwhile,
across the pond, I become a cookie, American-style.
I've got no problem with that. We biscuits adapt.

For when it comes down to the nitty-gritty,
have you seen a biscuit suffer a crisis of identity
whether I be *bis coctus*, cookie or plain old *bikkie*?

Yet of all my given names my personal favourite
is the *Empire Biscuit* which has a certain ring to it.
May the empire of a mouth crumble, as I do, to bits.

Meeting Old Father Thames

And so I came to a bridge called Westminster
arched over the Thames, London's pulse-beat water.
'So how are things?' I asked old Father Thames.
'Still living up to the sweet song of your name?'

And clearing his gurgle-deep-down liquid throat,
Father Thames said, 'Ah, well, *comme çi, comme ça*'
in a tone of voice that billowed real and raw
yet to my ear sounded strangely remote.

'Welcome to my well-trod guide book towpath.
Enjoy my shores,, stranger, whoever you be.
But pray, tell me, have you travelled from afar
just to take a selfie standing here beside me?'

I smiled: 'I'd like you, Father Thames, to be my mirror,
my eye, so to speak, into history's hidden corridors.
Father Thames grinned: 'You need look no further.
From Tide-End-Town, now Teddington, down I came

with mud on my hands...' Father Thames declaimed.
'I'm impressed,' I said. 'Not only are you good at rippling,
but I see you also have a grip on Empire's Kipling
whose *River's Tale* gave voice to your ebb and flow.'

I remember de bat-winged lizard birds
De Age of Ice and mammoth herds
When de giant tigers stalked dem down
From Regent's Park through to Camden Town...

Kipling uttered with a hint of Creole syncopation
brought a flush of colour to his wrinkling cheeks.
He sighed: 'Poems can always do with improvement.
And I'm inspired to give old Kipling some tweaks.

I, Thames, who girdled the battlements of Albion,
I, who witnessed Rome turn me to stamping ground,
past Westminster I also flowed with blood on my hands.
Not just mud, stranger. I repeat. Blood on my hands.

For I've seen the mudlarks, the downpressed poor,
scavenge their bread and butter from my shores,
And I can still hear those dark uprooted souls lament
for home-ground and kin in some other continent.

And still I flowed by the pedestalled on high –
cursed revenues still roosting on their statues.
And still I softly sang my sweet Thames song,
for I knew my place. Keep calm and ripple on.

Oh, those tourist folk who cruise my summer self,
if only they knew the half of my tainted depths.
Even my tides toss and turn in troubled conscience.
These nymphs (bless them) lull my turbulence.'

Old Father Thames looked suddenly distraught,
as if slavery had been all down to a river's fault.
So I did my very best to cheer the old boy up.
'Old Father Thames, I said, enough, chin up!

Chop-chop, old boy, pull yourself together.
Rivers shouldn't think too much. That's better.
Now look on the bright side of your estuary.
Seek deep in yourself for that which is holy.

For those pilgrim souls with India in their stride,
you'd be their far-from-home Ganges shrine,
though your tides unscroll a rippling reliquary
of bones unmourned, bones unlaid to rest.

My words were not intended to cause upset.
But Father Thames groaned his heaving breast
and said to me. 'Even as I hear your words,
stranger, my waves echo the unsung, the unheard.

But did you know that these waters of mine
were once a branch of the River Rhine?
For hundreds of miles to the East I flowed on
when old England and the Continent were one.

But from what I now hear the seagulls tell,
all's not well with our post-Brexit Channel...'
And leaning his brow on his Poseidon trident,
Old Father Thames seemed mortal as in bent.

To ease his tormented soul I spoke these words:
'You'll be pleased to know (just for the record)
for your size you're blessed with more bridges
than any other river anywhere in the world.

So listen to your bridges, old Father Thames.
Listen to that silent chorus of wood, iron, stone,
arching their torsos like visions of flesh and bone.
Open to the stride of the many as to the one.

Father Thames then lifted his eyes to the heavens
while I made for the tube. Brixton (as it so happens).

Pytheas the Greek in Britannia

But who in heaven's name you Brits might ask
was this foreigner by the name of Pytheas?

My detractors have dubbed me a hoaxster!
Fancy that! Me! A Greek migrant! An explorer

in whose veins still flows the blood of Homer
for I am no less than Pytheas of Massalia

(today's Marseille, France's multi-racial city,
that once paraded Apollo on its currency).

Thank God, I, Pytheas, did not live to see Apollo's
laurelled head usurped by the pound and euro

having myself passed on way back sometime BC.
So I don't expect you Brits have read my obituary.

Now the name Pytheas is the merest of footnotes.
Just another in Britannia's hall of forgotten ghosts.

But what if I said my eyes did spy the barbarians
when first I came upon the natives of Albion?

For the 'tattooed folk', as those Gauls were called,
did migrate as far as Atlantic-cradled Cornwall –

famous for its hobby-horsing and figgy-hobbin,
not to mention a bounteous supply of tin.

Legend has it fairies known as Knockers do abide
within the very bowels of the Cornish mines

and by their knocking warn of impending collapse,
But who's to tell the fiction from the facts?

Others claim these Knockers knock at mining shafts
to terrorise Man from disembowelling what's earth's.

And in my book, *On the Ocean*, I myself reflect
on what lurks beneath Poseidon's unfathomable depths.

What manner of beings exist to fuel Europe's fantasies
beyond Gibraltar (those Pillars of Hercules).

Published about 320 BC. Now out of print, alas!
But there was a time Alexandria's library knew Pytheas.

I, who had voyaged in a ship of hide and reeds,
without need for passport or proof of identity.

I, Pytheas, whose feet did tread the soil of Land's End
and saw tin-rich Cornwall fabled into Arthur's Tintagel.

Did I myself not encounter those painted Picts,
their skin inked with blue, keeping my gaze transfixed?

I who, staff in hand, did walk Blake's ancient Albion
before those Viking longships sniffed the horizon.

Back then Albion was all crooked lanes. No straight
roads till the Romans brought their concrete weight.

Yet, from the Great Beyond, I heard Africa's footfall,
when my ghost did meet a Black man in Cornwall.

Though uprooted from the dark cradle of his kin,
he did serenade my ears with his angelic violin.

The gentleman's name, I learnt, was Joseph Emidy.
One of the many who'd suffered an enforced odyssey.

Whether from Guinea, Brazil, the Caribee, Lisboa,
we exchanged nods as brother to brother.

Two ghosts who knew the meaning of diaspora.
Two disembodied beings well-met on Cornish ground –

the very ground that holds his bones six feet under,
Africa's son who'd led Truro's Philharmonic Orchestra.

Posterity informs me his compositions are lost.
But that violin spoke volumes of continents crossed

as I, Pytheas, do now speak. Yet another Other
in the chalky mosaic of Albion's migrant mirror.

The Migration of Coconut Water

(for Mark Hewitt, playwright, theatre-maker, friend, co-conspirator)

1

With a riddle
begins the tale
of a shell
but no snail

of a husk
but no corn

an oval
but no egg

milk-giver
but no cow

a mini-boat
its own transport

still no sign
of sail or oar

navigating continents
to seed new shores

turning bona fide
unsung resident.

Oh Coco Nucifera
I say hallelujah

to your cargo of nectar

2

One coconut both meat and drink,
in the words of Marco Polo,
centuries before Vita met Coco
promising 99% coconut water.
Where that missing percent gone
sounds like a trick question.
But if you really must know –
gone to pasteurisation.

3

Coconut water, you say?
Or did you mean that liquid sunshine
libating the valley of a throat?

Leave fancy sip-sip thru fancy straw
to dem straw-hat-tourists off cruise ship.
Man, tell me, where you born?

Don't tell me you never heard of the raw
communion with the jelly-blessed,
as in mouth-to-shell live and direct?

Is juice from heaven, yes.
The best partner to tango with a rum
on the dance-floor of the tongue.

4

All the while down memory lane
Harry Belafonte coconut woman
from that 50s hit still calling out,
every day you can hear her shout:

Get your coconut water
Man, it's good for yuh daughter
Coco got a lotta iron
Make you strong like a lion

now it's not in my place to question
whether this is myth or misconception,
but according to my grandmudda
coconut water can lead to conception.

5

Coconut water, yes,
first thing in the morning
last thing at night,
whether you black or white.
And is so I live to see
the day coconut water
(partially concentrate)
standing carton straight
on supermarket shelf
with sell-by date
come to colonise
a metropolitan palate.
A singular addition
to a plural
nation

(not to mention
warding off hypertension
or so I've been informed).

A far transatlantic cry
from the flickering memory
of that street corner sanctuary
presided over
by a votive vendor
beside a handcart,
cutlass priestly poised
to slice open
the head of paradise.

Coconut water, yes,
First thing in the morning
last thing at night,
whether you black or white.

We Mosquitoes

(calypso poem)

We mosquitoes we don't like to boast
we consider ourselves these islands' hosts,
we are original colonists
not by the sword by the proboscis.
We been around for millions of years,
and we ain't going nowhere, have no fear.
The ancient Egyptians tried fishing net,
they tried frankincense, we ain't extinct yet

> *Join in dis mosquito chorus*
> *buzz like you is one of us*
> *buzz buzz buzz buzz buzz buzz*
> *buzz buzz buzz buzz buzz buzz*

We like to bite democratically,
black, white, brown, we bite equally.
We don't agree with discrimination
we bite every pigmentation.
No, we mosquitoes we not prejudiced,
you could be a mister, you could be a miss,
one drop of blood is all we ask,
we ain't asking to fill a thermos flask

> *Join in dis mosquito chorus*
> *buzz like you is one of us*
> *buzz buzz buzz buzz buzz buzz*
> *buzz buzz buzz buzz buzz buzz*

Mosquito biting high, mosquito biting low,
from yuh head down to yuh Tobago.
Mosquito biting high, mosquito biting low,
from yuh armpit to yuh archipelago.

Dinosaur Dodo and dem gone
to a place called oblivion,
so we say bring on de pesticide
we mosquitoes have God on we side

    Join in dis mosquito chorus
    buzz like you is one of us
    buzz buzz buzz buz buzz buzz
    buzz buzz buzz buzz buzz buzz

Devon Jamboy Frederiksted, de Last
of de Danish West Indians

(Surprising as it may seem, the Danes, with their Danish West
India Company and a royal charter from the Danish King, did
manage in 1672 to set up a colony of Denmark on the Caribbean
island of St Thomas which later became part of the US Virgin
Islands)

Rumour 'bout town talk say him dead.
        No, not Devon Jamboy Frederiksted!

Him born-ground island St Thomas that once did fly
        de Danish flag under Caribbean sky.

But in Kingston JA him well and truly bred
        in de ways of youthman streetwise dread.

First name Devon signalling English kith and kin
        surname Frederiksted by dint of Viking

not to mention a generous helping
        of African blood in de cauldron of him skin.

But nickname does cling to you like clingfilm
        so by Jamboy all back-a-yard greet him.

Now mek me tell you how my heart just so miss a beat
        when one winter day who should I meet

out of de blue outside Paddington Station
        (and I swear to God was no apparition)

who else but swagger-stride Jamboy in de flesh.
        Tweed suit and tie, Jamboy dressed to kill, yes.

'Wha go on, bro?' him ask me. 'You act like you a-see ghost!
              Man, is I Jamboy self. Why you a-stare so?

After a heap of high-fiving on dat rush-hour platform
              I there and then made it my duty to inform

Jamboy that rumour-gram back in jamdown Kingston
              say him done dead and gone to de Great Beyond.

Jamboy buss out one laugh. 'So grapevine say I dead?
              But you a-talk to I, Devon Jamboy Frederiksted.

And since I name Devon after de English styling
              and titled Frederisksted via de Viking

I decide fe migrate England. Yes, I-man batten down
              inna corner of namesake clotted cream Devon.

Then a inner voice dat could only be Jah-Jah
              point a pathway to my own unsung saga.

And a-so I feel like lightning splitting open de head
              of I, Devon Jamboy Frederiksted.

But was only Viking Odin, de double-axe god, opening de way
              back to me 33 percent Danish DNA.

Then enlightenment strike I like Selassie hand.
              Since Viking chart whale-road to dis-ya England

'bout time I Jamboy claim piece mih Viking inheritance.
              My kenning kindred been here before Saxon advance.

No true? Yeah man...so see I Jamboy a-forward into de future
              like I-man is comeback Ashanti Viking warrior...'

But Jamboy words left me stone-speechless.
          Like they coming from the mouth of a man possessed.

And all I could think of telling Jamboy was 'walk good'
          as me watch him step light amidst a grey crowd.

Ice Speaks

Must I remind short-memoried humankind
of a once-upon-a-woolly-mammoth time,
when my permafrost embraced continents?

My ghostly glaciers extending their grimace
to white-out a Neanderthal dawn
and do my bit for what's called extinction.

But let me say, I'm not all doom and gloom.
No, I do have my chilled-out moments.
Like when I become the crystal sediments

cushioned in your cocktail glass,
the chorus in your lemonade,
the loud castaway in your rum.

Now it saddens me to see talking primates
skating their span of time on thin ice
(to borrow a common idiom)

for when the day of reckoning comes
and my melting cap doffs its sub-zero self,
prepare your high-rise stone to weep upon

my lap of water rising by the hourglass.
But under my hard edges I'm a real softie.
For what are freak floods and tsunamis

if not my tears returning home to roost?
Yes, my leviathan grief seeking out the crevices
of your fading green. So disturb my frozen sleep

and I, Ice, will release the weeping god of me.

The Murmur of the Forest in an Adjective
(for Ruben Dario, 1867-1916)

'We must remember that he was a stranger from an
undeveloped land, that he had Indian blood in his veins and
lacked the complexity and the sophistication which would
belong to a European of his gifts and tastes.'

(An Oxford don's response to the Nicaraguan poet)

As undeveloped yes as a 3-D Olmec pyramid
that would dazzle the geometry of Euclid.
You, Dario, prodigy of word and vision,
no stranger to the heart's bridging horizon
the aroma of a star, the colour of a sound,
a trans-world whiff of Olympian ambrosia
blowing across the sierras of Meso-America.

Of you sweet ill-fated Lorca once said
Dario puts the murmur of the forest in an adjective
you who were a student of the clouds
you who would take questions from a swan
a mind marinated in the cosmopolitan
you who saw in the condor over the Andes
Walt Whitman's eagle's still-gliding wheel

In your own words, plural has been
the celestial story of your heart
Plural ha sido la celeste/ historia de mi corazón
each soul *a universo de universos/*universe of universes.
And the Indian blood coursing through your veins
stays faithful to the wind's feathered refrain
of Moctezuma shedding drops of doom

of Atahualpa fading under an Inca moon.
Yet you planted Parnassus in your history's bed of pain
and Pan mounted the ladder of a Mayan flute
while Mallarmé's music sounded in an Aztec rain.
As ever astonished by the soul of things
balanced between cathedral and pre-Columbian
you put to your ear a global seashell.

So let an Oxford don think what an Oxford don thinks.
You poeta, won't question your inner sphinx.

Saluting Derek

(for Derek Walcott, 1930-2017)

It's not these onions that trigger the tears
on this March Friday of Lent 2017
overshrouded by England's sun-shy clouds

not these onions I'm in the middle of peeling
but the news of your passing (Derek gone)
that spills my thoughts into eye-water's ovation

to your pen dipped in the ink of horizons
to your lines limboing their tight timber
for a brood of metaphors to nest in

your green syllables still echoing a leaf
your eye tuned to a raindrop's salutation
and though the immortelle needs no ambassador

you would choose to voice its scarlet to the world
as you did for the water-cradled canna lily
as you did for the conch shell's wordless word

and though the conch shell can speak for itself
today its spiral tongue chooses to be silent
and like those Royal Palms at royal half-mast

may the canefields hoist their nine-night vigil
the poinsettia bleed the petals of your name
the blue hills over Castries put on their sad best

may the sea-grape salute you in the salt of its patois
the hibiscus wake to your everlasting sleep
the bougainvillea's thorns crown your going

may the frigate bird cross itself in condolence
the lizard bask on a branch of mourning
the tree-frog toll its bell at the very least

Caribbean genius, you said in your Nobel speech,
must be allowed the gift of contradiction.
(Or sentiments more or less to that effect.)

You who dared assemble fragments of epic
out of Empire's lingering legacy.
Antillean bard, your epitaph, is the sea's script.

Walt

Bravo to that prodigal day of summer 1855,
 when leaves of grass became eurekas of light,
 and you, Walt Whitman, loafed and swayed
 to the bounty of being alive

your hat, cocked to the holy now,
 not losing sleep over the how
 or for that matter the why –
 content just to breathe in sky

to chill out on a spear of grass
 which you in memorable metaphor hailed
 as God's dropped handkerchief –
 a token of common trodden-on grace

embracing in your worship the most ordinary
 as worthy of a line of rhapsody
 discovering in the mouse's minute squeak
 a miracle to stagger the cynical quintillions

and by noonday by nightfall bursting into praise
 you said clear and sweet is my soul
 and clear and sweet is all
 that is not my soul…open to the call

of beast on four legs, bird on wing,
 of sea-creature, creeping thing,
 upright speaking man, woman, child,
 from far-flung unsung quarters

encompassing race and gender
 inviting the globe to your bosom-bone
 all the goodness of earth and sun
 all the goodness of sky and moon.

Hoeing your patch of onions
        you become Zen monk and nun rolled into one.
        Merging time-bound self with timeless Self
        you turn Hindu bridging atman to Brahman

to the body-brimming streets of Manhattan.
        So keep on loafing, brother Whitman,
        you can't go wrong with the universe in your tongue.
        A multitude of contradictions your travelling companion.

Dear Michael

*(for Michael Gilkes, 1933-2020,
poet, playwright, beloved sixth-form teacher)*

For me you are always my Sir.
That back-in-the-sixties teacher
to sunny-eyed adolescents.
You, our homegrown shepherd
before a sixth-form blackboard –
a flock of young Guyana souls
taking notes on Joyce's epiphanies –
Portrait of the Artist as a Young Man,
an exam text set from overseas,
Dublin not exactly a stone's throw
to Georgetown's Dutch-built canals
almost bridal with canna lilies.

You, the ever-light-touch scholar
with the pointy Elizabethan beard,
captain of a classroom flagship
connecting dispossessed Caliban
to the indigenous Carib-an,
that Amerindian sounding
to this day haunting
the corridors of my tongue.

But more than teacher,
you'd also tread the boards
of the old Theatre Guild,
sword-wielding in Hamlet's leotards.
Add to this your playwright's pen
re-inhabiting the hammock
of Couvade (your staged homage
rebirthing pre-Columbian ritual).

Guyana's rainforest labyrinth
the arteries of your inner map,
following you wherever
you choose to transplant
that beautiful mind of yours.

So what now, Michael, Sir,
but turn to your love poem
for your piano-playing Joan
of 33 Barrack Street, Kingston,
colonial-styled with that iconic
wooden bottom-house
where you'd wheel your bicycle
like your wheeling heart –
not forgetting that seawall-facing
lighthouse swivelling its beams
towards Atlantic's dark archives,
probing the mind's invisible skyline
like a good teacher's beacon eye.

A Farewell to Poet James Berry's Hat

Contrary to Western opinion,
hats are capable of abstract thought.
So what is that hat thinking?
What's going through the head of that hat

perched headless on a cushion of flowers
that crown the coffin of James Berry?
More a dapper gesture for his final ship
of wicker ready for infinity.

Anchored deep in thought, that hat thinks.
Where's that brown dome I once shaded?
That bald head no more my global friend?
That shining orb it was my job to cradle?

Of course, the hat keeps such thoughts to itself.
Resigned to silence under its dapper brim.
Yet that hat now feeling more than honoured
to have nested on the head of Jim-Jim

that hat that throbbed to the pulse of his words
now doffing itself to eternity's applause.

Gone But Still Spring Cleaning

(for Jean Binta Breeze, 1956-2021)

How too soon your *is*
has been googled into *was*

Your brackets closed.
Your obits big and bold.

Yet the tongue of my mind
rejoices in uttering your name

that brings a Caribbean breeze
to keep heartbeat well-timed

to the rustling anthems
of palm trees on eternal standby

the Atlantic's raving riddims
grounding your inner ear

between your Jamaica sanctuary
and adopted Leicestershire county

with its *me duck* salutation
warming you to the Midlands idiom

yet rooted to apron strings evenings
your mother's honey your balm of Gideon.

Gone but still spring-cleaning
the cobwebs that lace the ceiling

of transatlantic history.
And now from a veranda beyond our seeing

that must be you strutting sky's blue stage
showing how love outweighs rage

showing how bright-eyed dreaming
can redress old wounds in rebel wings.

Three Siblings of the Word

Meet three siblings of the Word,
the Brontë lasses whose quills ventured
upwards from the blank of a page,
yet rooted to a hilltop parsonage
among these moors that beckon surrender.

There's our Emily letting her mind roam
in the middle of household chores.
She won't allow baking to distract her
from the slow rising of chapter into chapter.
Yes, caught up in her own plot,

Emily's daydreaming of God knows what
fictional twist of heart or dicey fate –
A world away from small globes of cup cakes.
You can expect, even mid-embroidery,
to lose our Emily to authorial reverie.

Of course, never in her wildest imagining,
would she have catered for a futuristic
Kate Bush scaling her wuthering heights
all the way to top of the popping heights –
a barefoot siren in balletic flight.

All the while, there's big sis, Charlotte,
occupied with laying out the cutlery,
and there's Anne, thinking wrongly or rightly,
that when women tread male-run territory,
a manly pseudonym would ring no feminine bell.

And so the clergyman's youngest daughter
slips into her pen-name Mr Acton Bell.
And quoting more or less of Charlotte's words:
Prejudice settles in the soil of the bones,
taking root as firm as weeds among stones

unless loosened and fertilised
by an education that sees in common
human ore the soul's hidden diamond.
Meanwhile, the gleaming ghost of mahogany
keeps vigil over the imagination's flesh.

Mahogany, resigned to being a writing desk,
still feels in the shine of its veins the memory
of how gods fall when a forest is ravaged.
If Jamaica's *Swietenia mahagoni* grows extinct,
here in Haworth village mahogany cradles page,

an inspired pen about to be dipped into ink.
But in the dark mirror of a mahogany desk,
no intrusive ghosts from a colony dispossessed.
Only a flickering candle the silent sentinel
to the birth pangs of a classic in progress.

And back to musing in a Victorian chair,
Charlotte sits there polishing her *Jane Eyre*
who will direct a blind and troubled gent
towards her own soul-mate light – one Rochester.
But Charlotte's thoughts are beyond a bestseller.

Now, all you who pass that hilltop parsonage,
pause a while in what's known as Brontë country.
Not far a black body once made a run for liberty.
Take heed, tourist, centuries later you might be one
who hears these moors speaking a plural tongue.

This Creature Known as Michael Rosen

(for Mike the Man)

Let's go, not on a bear hunt,
let's go on a Michael Rosen hunt.

Follow the tracks up your heart's mountain.
Not a bad place to start poet-hunting.

There you'll encounter a singular creature
who lets words be his rabbi teacher.

Be warned, this creature known as Michael Rosen
is not the kind you'll find posing

a box ordained by the one-stream mainstream.
After all, he's got his mum's and dad's socialist genes.

No surprise the Vietnam War had fired his protest.
The grail of justice his lifelong quest despite arrest.

Or like that time some Oxford hairdresser refused
to cut black people's hair. Michael placarded his views

of how prejudice can put on a subtle face
to ensure the *us* and *them* be kept in place.

You Harrow-born boy with horizons in your pocket,
wordplay your mind-opening rocket.

In the grown-up playground of your imagination
the child in you still skips to the turn of a song,

a schoolyard chant, a Yiddish joke, timelessly cracked
beyond the borders of the Union Jack

because you Michael being Michael long cherished
the gift of breath as uncounted harvest.

And now more than ever with Emma at your side
reaping hope from the vineyard of an open mind.

Namaste Mr Lear

O how lovely to meet you, Mr Lear,
you who so sensibly held nonsense dear.
For in nonsense, pure and absolute,
you found wisdom's foolproofious truth.

Foolproofious? A real word? Or a made-up one
to enliven the legs of the legless lexicon?
But under skies where the tall kamamahs grew,
sheltering from the monsoon (as you do)

you, a peaceful man preparing to kill time,
heard inwardly the bells of nonsense chime.
Suddenly, out of the downpouring blue
you began outwardly pouring a verbal brew

of English lingo spiced with a dollop of Hindi
to describe that mysterious roaming beastie
you'd call the Cummerbund (from kamarband)
which the Hindus use for sash or waistband.

And by flight of nonsensically poetic liberty,
you'd conjure an ayah (Hindi for a nanny)
into that perching specimen – the ayah bird.
And the dhobie (another Hindi word

for the workaday washer-man who
sun-dries clothes on a pole of bamboo)
has become a sittable cushion to lie on,
just in case that horrid Cummerbund

(whatever gender he or she might be)
comes to swallow your anonymous anatomy.
And can that be the jampan, an old sedan chair,
howling a melody from its meloobrious lair?

If nonsense turns one's senses sensibly round,
who would choose to be senselessly square?
So again, how lovely to meet you, Mr Lear,
and shake you by your broodydicious beard.

Broodydicious? Is that a word I made up?
Better check your spellcheck downwardly up.

While on a journey across India (1873-75) Edward Lear of 'The Owl and the
Pussycat' fame delighted in the sounds of Hindi words. He even took poetic
liberties, giving some his trademark nonsense twist.

My Little Guy, Says Edith Fawkes:
Bereaved Mother of Guy Fawkes Addresses the Press

He'll always be my little Guy,
Crooned him many a lullaby.
I still see him so cutesome in his cot.
A thousand winks from a gunpowder plot.

Ever a shy child, and so sensitive.
What was he doing in a bloody cellar
with all those bloody explosives?
Bad company, that's what, I tell yar.

Always told him, stay clear of fire, son,
fire means Hell to good Catholics.
Never guessed he'd grow up with ambition
for what clever folk them call Pyrotechnics.

But come November fifth, when bonfires rage,
it's my little Guy what takes centre stage.

Monsieur Voltaire Commits a *Faux Pas* in 18th-century England

Louis-le-Grand, the Parisian Jesuit College
(France's Eton for the crème de la crème)
that had produced the likes of Molière,
would also produce yours truly Voltaire.
My career, you could say, was volatile.

I'm at that point in my life, dear reader,
when I'm about to embark for exile
in England – makes a pleasant change
from that wretched cell in la Bastille
where I'd spent two years imprisoned.

My self-righteous accusers say I'm guilty
of seasoning reason with rhyme
and subjecting rhyme to reason.
Yet, when the guillotine begins to beckon,
we lose rhyme and reason. Or so I reckon.

In England it was my fervent hope
to meet Jonathan Swift and Alexander Pope,
two kindred satire-tongued blokes
(to borrow the English expression)
who wrap their stinging barbs in jokes.

I'd been charmed by Swift's tale of Gulliver,
and with equal relish had mulled over
Pope's biting wit couched in couplets:
As in – *I am His Highness' dog at Kew.*
Pray tell me, Sir, whose dog are you?

My English, you'll note, dear reader,
is improving minute by minute.
So is my tolerance – a habit
the English are known to perfect,
I might add, also minute by minute.

The way they polish their displeasure
with measured dollops of restraint
never fails to tickle this foreigner.
No doubt a nation of philosophers
would be my humble summing up.

They pour their traumas into tea cups
as they do their weather grievances.
In this they have made great advances.
And by keeping calm and carrying on
they stem the stride of Revolution.

Voilà the English, *voilà les Anglais!*
In my book on England I plainly state
that the English can teach us French
a thing or two about free speech.
In Paris that didn't go down too well.

They burnt my book in fires of hell.
So what if my pen thinks and writes
like a free Englishman? *C'est la vie!*
Blame my pen for dipping itself
in the English ink of liberty.

That being said, I have a confession.
Once I did upset my English hostess
by managing to commit a *faux pas*
(or to use another English expression)
I was well out of order! I guess I was.

I'd said Shakespeare had taken liberties
with Aristotle's classical unities
of time, place and action. Oh dearie me!
The lady's features seemed non-plussed
when I called the Bard's Hamlet barbarous.

Yet, being of free-thinking English mindset,
she complimented me on my rashness.
Then whispered, placing to her lips a serviette,
'I so happen to have two tickets for *King Lear*,
don't suppose you'd care to join me, Monsieur Voltaire?'

How very English of her I found myself thinking,
while the Frenchman in me refrained from winking.

Glorious Uncertainty in de Bedroom

(calypso poem)

(spoken)
When cricket laws enter bedroom privacy,
prepare yuhself for amorous uncertainty.
Leh me tell you 'bout a certain umpire
who couldn't let go even after he retired.
He'd dress up for bed like he is a Dicky Bird.
See he in he white coat surveying de bedroom,
ready as ever to raise that finger of doom

He'd tell he wife 'when ah touch me leg like so,
that mean leg-bye, darling, Ah want you to know.
When Ah stretch two hand like so horizontally,
dat mean de ball too wide, even fractionally.
When ah raise two hand like so up to de ceiling,
I ain't playing some seagull about to start wheeling,
no, darling, is a big six, de maximum, I signalling.'

(chorus/calypso tempo)
> *umpire by day-o*
> *umpire by night-o*
> *he mind only on*
> *de leather and willow*
> *umpire by day-o*
> *umpire by night-o*
> *even when he wife*
> *turn off de light-o*

(spoken)
De wife, expecting romance, now starting to fidget.
Hubbie busy twiddling wid he little light gadget.
He monitoring de condition of de weather,
but de wife approaching de end of she tether.

He say, 'darling, tonight is a special occasion.
Our golden anniversary. Yes, time is getting on,
but I'll wait for you in de square leg position.'

Suddenly, see he by de wardrobe crouching down,
pretending like he chasing a intruder pigeon.
He wife she thinking to sheself (and quite rightly)
dis umpire ting like it got he flighty-flighty.
So she decide to humour hubbie and play along
by slipping into she shortie flannel white nightgown.
That little number does never fail to turn him on.

(chorus/calypso tempo)
>*umpire by day-o*
>*umpire by night-o*
>*he mind only on*
>*de leather and willow*
>*umpire by day-o*
>*umpire by night-o*
>*even when he wife-o*
>*put on she flannel white-o*

(spoken)
Hear he: 'Dat flannel white does tingle mi spine,
but remember is no-ball if yu foot cross de line.
All my life to fair-play I've been committed,
though tonight ball-tampering will be permitted.
But if we is to play de Englishman game lawfully.
then two intervals must be called accordingly,
so, darling, how say we call a interval fo' tea?'

Hear she: 'Honey, de ball old but de pitch still turning.
And as you can see, I ready to reverse my swing?
For God sake, man, we ain't got whole night,
I starting to perspire in all dis flannel white.
At dis rate I go have to appeal for light!'

Hear he: 'Appeal upheld. A timely intervention.
Play will be suspended until further inspection.'

(chorus/calypso tempo)
    umpire by day-o
    umpire by night-o
    he mind only on
    de leather and willow
    umpire by day-o
    umpire by night-o
    even when he wife
    appeal fo' light-o

Bards in White Flannels

Here's to those postcolonial Bards in white flannels
wielding the willow like their consonants and vowels,
spicing the English tongue with bouncing syncopation
reversing the swing of adverbs into wayward verbs.

Well-groomed in the ways of glorious uncertainty,
see how they stride the turf of Empire's legacy
raising their bats to the protocol of the Canon
while hooking beyond the boundary any loose noun.

They've learnt from pitches that syntax too can crack.
The thing is to keep the wicket of the soul intact,
not flashing at tempting black and white slogans,
not letting history's wounds halt the harvest of runs

but acknowledging the heart's global pavilion,
rejoicing at the crease in commonwealth communion.

Bowdlerising the Bard

To delete or not to delete
that is the delicate question.
But even the Bard of Avon,
we daresay can be improved on.
However timeless his timely lines,
I, Thomas Bowdler, and my dear sister,
will attempt to make them more refined.

Now, let's start with Lady Macbeth's
manic outburst *Out damned spot!*
Sorry, Bard, but we'll have that replaced
with *Out crimson spot!*
Damned spot is definitely not
in the daintiest of Christian taste.

As for Romeo and Juliet,
all those veiled references to sex
are very far from child-friendly.
The bawdy hand of the dial
is now upon the prick of noon!
No, no, *the prick of noon* just won't do,
whatever Mercutio's point of view.

Isn't *upon the point of noon*
more (shall we say) palatable
for juvenile minds round the table?
The Bard himself will no doubt agree
(for the sake of moral correctness)
that our bowlderised version
is better suited for all the family.

Thomas Bowdler (1754–1825) was an English physician who, with his editor sister Henrietta Maria Bowdler, decided to publish a cleaned-up version of the works of Shakespeare. Without intending, the Bowdlers, by their 'bowdlerising', entered the dictionary.

Viagra in Me Cocoa

(calypso poem)

(spoken)
Dorothy, I beg you please, be gentle with me,
Remember, I'm eighty-two going on eighty-three.
Dorothy, I beg you please, be gentle with me,
these days Papa Joe have to take things slow,
these days this Papa too old to play Romeo.
But I never say no to a nice hot cocoa

She say, 'I have just de ting to make you frisky,
scientists say it is de drug of de century
Viagra in your cocoa is de kind of nightcap
that will make Papa Joe old wings start to flap.'
I said, 'My dear, are you out of your mind?
You know I don't touch drugs of any kind!'

She say 'don't worry, your secret safe with me.
Papa Joe, you just lie back, mek yuself comfy.
I'll do de honours and bring you nice hot cocoa.'
Soon Dorothy in de kitchen doctoring de cocoa.
'Drink up, Papa Joe, dis cocoa does do de trick.
Dis cocoa does mek old firewood ketch quick.'

(sung calypso tempo with audience joining in)
    Dorothy, what you put in dis cocoa,
    I don't know fo' sure,
    but tell me why you close de bedroom door?
    Dorothy, my plan was to gracefully age,
    I hope dis cocoa don't send me to me grave

(spoken)

Well, I sipped away, if I may say, cautiously,
till Ah could feel a tingle all down to me knee.
My pressure rose, I thought my heart would fail.
To steady mihself, I held on to de bedrail.
To her question 'how you feeling down below?'
I confessed down below was starting to glow.

Now, sadly, my friends, I have to relate
what Dorothy cocoa did to my heart rate.
In short, her caress led me to cardiac arrest.
I breathe my last breath in Dorothy nightdress.
Here in heaven they feed me milk and honey,
but heaven with no cocoa ain't heaven for me.

(sung calypso tempo)

> *St Peter, take back yuh halo*
> *and give me a taste of Dorothy cocoa*
> *St Peter, take back yuh halo*
> *and give me a taste of Dorothy cocoa.*

Erasmus in England, 1499

I'll skip over, if I may,
my burial in Basle Minster,
the Swiss air my unseen pallbearer,
            1536 the year my brackets closed.

Rewind to my time-free repose
in a doctor's daughter's womb,
seeded by a Catholic priest.
            Out of wedlock, if you please.

Pronounced illegitimate
but thankfully literate,
my early days groomed by Latin schooling.
            Fast forward to Paris for tutoring.

Though my vows of chastity
had voided conjugal proximity,
that didn't stop me conjugating
            verbs from Greek and Latin.

My birthplace, Rotterdam, shrouded
by then in toddling memory,
my birth date also somewhat clouded.
            But 1466 will do me nicely.

One of my English students was the aptly
titled Lord William Mountjoy
for whom mounting horses
            was indeed a great joy.

Oh dear! Did I just say mounting?
Not exactly in the best possible taste.
So with tasteful haste
            shall we say galloping

gave Lord Mountjoy much delight?
And he it was who did invite
this Catholic to England in 1499.
                    (The weather futuristically fine.)

By then Michelangelo had miracled
a block of stone into his *Pietà* –
the crucified Jesus cradled by a mother
                    like a pierced flower

not forgetting old Dürer's *Four*
Horsemen of the Apocalypse
showing how a Renaissance engraving
                    can preserve death's foregone eclipse.

But I promise not to be morbid.
So onto more merry matters.
During my sojourn in England I encountered
                    the young Prince Henry

who would grow up to be
a serial be-header
Of course, I'd never have guessed
                    the cherubic nine-year-old tootling

his descant recorder like a snake charmer
would turn out the way he did.
I did, however, enjoy the companionship
                    of Thomas More (later Henry's advisor).

More shared with me his dream
of Utopia – a world better known as ideal.
All the more a cold stroke of irony
                    that More (echoing *moria*, the Greek for folly)

should also lose his sober head to the folly
of the aforementioned King Henry,
who happened to be a bit of a Reformer.
                    If he had his reforming way

he'd have the Pope's head on a silver slab.
The Reformation, you could say,
was King Henry's royal form of rehab.
                    But that's off the record.

Folks who know me know how I feel
on the subject of Kings, Queens,
Barons, Pontiffs, Judges who preen
                    their inner wolf in sheep's clothing.

For such kind I mix my loathing
with a pinch of Lucian banter.
I'd much rather the company
                    of the King's jester-in-residence.

The Fool's nonsense to me makes more sense.
Or in the words of Euripides,
the Fool is known to speak folly,
                    but the Wise Man has two tongues.

One with which to speak truth.
One with which to speak to the occasion
for a standing ovation,
                    his demeanour visibly meek.

Moderns call this double-speak.
Double-speak indeed! In that case, give me
a double dose of the Fool's folly.
                    If I must bow, I'll bow to buffoonery.

The Fool's Yule

No gleam of gold
no breath of frankincense
no balm of myrrh

None of these have I
for I am neither
King nor wise

I'm only a Fool
in love with giving
at this season of Yule

Therefore shall I seek
that newborn babe
swaddled in straw

No star in the East
shall this Fool follow
but the compass of my nose

And no gift shall I bring
but a sprig of holly
to crown his glory

And red berries of course
to teach the little one
his first lesson

in the brightness of blood.
So shall this Fool adore
the child's evergreen soul.

In Your Hands

Who am I? Here's a clue. In your hands I reside.
I'm there where friendship and gratitude abide.

When signatures command the dotted line,
I'm the gesture by which agreements are defined.

I can be taboo but I'm not pass my sell-by date.
If you haven't guessed yet, my name is Handshake.

Been there among Stone Age dwellers with no wheel.
But coming to grips with me was no big deal.

Been there when the Neanderthals got convivial.
I'm talking millions of years from the digital.

Been there to see Heracles reach out to Pholus.
One a Greek hunk. The other half-man, half-horse.

Been there when the Romans became matey
with the stranger. Now friend. Once enemy.

Been there in the green heart of the Amazon
when feathered humans touched skin one-to-one.

Been there centre-stage for many a photo-op
when politicians seize the moment to appear on top.

And didn't I join King Shalmaneser, the Assyrian,
with King Marduk Zakir-Shumi, the Babylonian?

Wasn't I there at the time of the Black Death
when the plague put a sudden stop to breath?

Wasn't I there at the scourge of the Spanish flu
long before the rise of the *man-sized tissue*.

And now a pandemic makes touching touch-and-go,
I'll be there disguised this time as an elbow.

THE PLANTS ARE STAYING PUT

This Thing Called Gardening

1 *Time-in*

So you decide to have a go
at this thing called gardening.
So far so good. Why not begin
with a bolder than bold lupin?
And with so tipple-evoking a name
as (wait for it) *Tequila Flame*,
better make that a double lupin.

2 *Reviving the Latin Tongue*

As stay-at-home garden beginner
envious of the green-fingered,
I take some consolation
from reviving the Latin tongue.
Even your fast wilting failure
may start to sound like a success,
if with a certain Ciceronian stress
you were to exclaim to a visitor:
'A shame, it never took off,
my *salvia coronaria*.
The same goes, I'm afraid,
for my *iris matinata*.
Next time I'll try organic compost.
But I'm keeping my fingers crossed
for my *cynara cardunculus*.
Before you know it, you'll be sounding
like a posh Roman with an Oxford lisp.

3 *Allium Schuberti*

And when your *allium schubertii*
raises its chalice
of purple-tinted spikes,
what's there not to like?

4 *Never Too Late for a Pot*

Is the garden south-facing?
Was that the question?
I thought you'd never ask.
O where's that bloody compass?
Never around when you need it.
I guess I'll settle for pot luck
as in terracotta. That would do.
Yes, whatever the direction
that happens to be on offer
(partial shade, full sun, whatever)
it's reassuring to remember –
never too late for a pot to learn
to do a sudden U-turn.

5 *In flagrante*

Would I stand accused as a voyeur
if I should happen to spy on
a bee in mid-flight bottom
topping a lupin's petalled boudoir?
In that case I'll be discreet.
Observe the ground-cover at my feet.
Pretend indifference to their carrying on
their oh-so *in flagrante* shenanigan.

6 Hydrangea

Did you just say mopheads?
That's no way to refer to
Hydrangea Macrophylla Hortensias!
The pink-bouffant-styled prima donna
rising to her inner extravaganza.
Then again, to be fair,
maybe the human-polluted air
could do with a bit of mopping.
In case Mother Nature should pop in.

7 Honeysuckle

Thank you, climbers,
for scaling that faceless wall
in pilgrim-petalled footsteps.
Yes, that grey concrete grimace
could do with a silent chuckle
of pink-lipped honeysuckle.

8 Sedum

Branded 'the stone crop'.
An in-joke shared
by gardening buffs.
Only a stone, they declare,
requires less care.
But Sedum isn't fussed
by facing north or south.
Partial to shade and sun,
Sedum spreads itself
with sweet abandon,
grateful for any position.

Low maintenance
is what comes to mind.
A plant after my own heart.
Forgiving even to those
who, for better or for worse,
forget the meaning of thirst.

9 *Fig*

What would Adam and Eve
have thought of the freshly
potted fig tree on my patio?
Basking in bare-limbed memory
of what they'll learn to call libido,
would they have been impressed
by my fig's fledgling greenery?
Or dismissed it as too modest
for their discovered modesty?

10 *The Margin*

To this poet's eye –
giving gardening a try –
the empty border
can be classified
as the margin
of a page of earth
begging to be filled in
with shade-loving fern.
Perhaps a Japanese acer
with its autumn treasury?
One of those shadies
according to the manual.

On the other hand, what if
the unattended marginal
should remain perennial?
As in left free to breathe.

11 *Fingers Crossed*

When your trailing geranium
is doing just that –
trailing far behind.
And your hardy perennial
is proving to be neither
hardy nor perennial.
Is this when you despair?
No, time for a silent prayer
that in the long long run,
your Kenyan runner beans
at least manage a marathon.

12 *Salsa Chili*

Once you're in the groove
there's no stopping your moves.
How your purple waistline,
ever so slowly unwinds
to some driving inner beat.
On the tongue's dance-floor,
that's where you flaunt your heat.

13 *Seed*

Learn fast how a seed
refuses to be hurried
into bud-bright form.
Content to pace itself
like a micro batsman
with all of the time
in the world to wait
for the well-timed
stroke of revelation –
already bloom-primed
for its own silent ovation.

Weeds

For just happening to be
in the wrong place
you are well maligned

labelled parasite
invader trespasser
in short non grata

the unwelcome guests
with no plan to depart
in the near future.

The laidback scroungers
who make their bed
wherever they creep.

But with such poetic
names to live up to,
you have nothing to prove

but unwind your thriving plot
where you ought not
(like that lawn where you intrude).

Crabgrass, Goosegrass,
Quackgrass (whatever name
you choose to bind and abide by)

wasn't it a blade of grass
that old Whitman rhapsodised
as the handkerchief of the Lord?

As far as metaphors go,
that's certainly arresting,
but even God's handkerchief

shouldn't be seen waving
through cracks in one's decking
or pride-of-joy crazy paving

not to mention hyjacking
one's Zen-inspired pathway,
its gravel now the backing

for your foreground breeding.
But is it wise to uproot
your silent parable

of live and again let live?
See how the very stones
are more than content

to forget and forgive –
rubbing easy shoulders
with your green insurgence.

The Plants Are Staying Put

1

Rewind to old Darwin beside his *Mimosa Pudica*,
hoping to stimulate the plant's inner
mojo with a riff or two from his bassoon.
A little, shall we say, homespun experiment.
But his prickly *Mimosa Pudica* remained unimpressed
by the clownish capers and quavers of the instrument.
No surprise there. Darwin should have known better
than to go testing the sensory nerves of a plant
that folk call by the common name, *Touch-me-not*.
A shy creeper. An introvert. Sensitive to contact.
(And that includes a sudden bassoon attack.)
Now I'm starting to have second thoughts
about introducing my bashful dwarf lily
to a blast of Beethoven's Fifth Symphony.

2

Now fast-track to the current climate
of self-isolation. A globe gathered in a viral web.
Sorrow has sprouted cross-border legs.
But the plants are staying put. Nowhere
to go but as far as their roots permit.
Do they as well sense lockdown in the air?
See how the campanula in the wind's caress
silently prepares its fanfare of tiny blue bells
to applaud the hands that bring care to distress.
Even the hydrangea, known for its brashness,
now nods a Pentecostal purple with quiet gravitas.
And keeping much more than a minute's silence.
Perhaps its way of telling us to be each other's
gardener. Trusting in the heart's persistent flower.

Lewes to London Post-lockdown

Sun-splintered slate-coloured clouds parade
their ambivalence on this day of May 2021
over the first stop after Lewes – Plumpton –
telling me now I'm well and truly bound
for the Big Smoke (good old London) –
my first excursion post-lockdown.

Back in March 2020 life was maskless
and a hug yet not something you'd best
avoid (a hug having evolved to a time bomb).
There's no denying an embrace can be nice.
But following the Government's advice,
better not be in a hurry to be too cosy

which can endanger both hugger and huggee.
Then out of the ether a disembodied reminder
to wear a face covering unless exempt.
For a moment I swore I'd heard unless unkempt.
Not the best of acoustics on a train on the move,
even for travellers not unkempt but well-groomed.

There goes that voice again, this time reminding...
Please mind the gap between the train and platform...
Oh when last have I heard those words? Such soothing
music to my stay-at-home ears... I can't believe
we're actually approaching Haywards Heath.
Is this a dream? Some masked soul pinch me please.

Next stop: Gatwick Airport. A pregnant absence
of passengers wheeling wheelies with the ebullience
of holidaymakers anticipating somewhere foreign.
Now satellite dishes, church spires, scaffolding,
foretell the expected coming into East Croydon,
which after so long begins to sound like Elysium.

Presuming that Clapham Junction hasn't relocated
that should be our next stop. One tunnel later,
a graffiti-scarred overhead bridge, excavated
earth heaped like some inner city concrete hillock,
reassures me Clapham Junction is where I last left it.
We're making good time. Exactly 10.23 by the clock.

Due for Victoria Station at precisely 10.29,
unless there's some virus on the tracks, or divine
intervention in the form of the wrong kind of snow.
With the train changing to that slow-down tempo,
past a fleeting Chelsea Bridge, its metal torso
still gleaming, Victoria waiting like a long lost friend.

And with the Thames rippling my mind, I wend
my way for a ritualistic roll-up and pint of Guinness
at the pub just over the road. Gasping...in suspense...
The pub saluting Stratford's son, *The Shakespeare*,
shut tight! Even the The Boozing Bard alas speechless!
But you're still there, London. Deserted. But still there.

CASANOVA THE PHILOSOPHER

Casanova lives to challenge convictions. With the joyful impertinence of a commedia dell'arte character, he reverses the established order, pokes fun at identities, and blurs the boundaries of certainty.

LYDIA FLEM, *Casanova, or, The Art of Happiness*

Casanova would be bemused to discover that he is remembered today almost exclusively for his sex life. He was a fiercely proud intellectual and polymath, who worked at different times as a violinist, soldier, alchemist, faith-healer, and even librarian, and originally trained to be a priest.

IAN KELLY, *Casanova*

In recalling the pleasures I enjoyed, I relive them, while I laugh at the pains I endured and no longer feel. A member of the universe, I speak to the air and fancy myself giving an account of my conduct of affairs the way a major-domo does to his master before retiring. As for my future, I have never, as a philosopher cared to worry much about it, since I can know nothing about it...

GIACOMO CASANOVA, *The Story of My Life*

1 *A Rake?*

I, Giacomo Casanova, ought to sue the dictionary
that defines a casanova as a womanising rake,
a ne'er-do-well libertine who shuns matrimony,
one who utters smoothie flatteries that are fake –
mere playboy chitchat angling for a one-night stand.
If that's your casanova, then I'm not your man.
Call me a compulsive gambler with a mind intent
on mounting the ladder of the social lottery.
But a rake? After a common garden implement?
No, when a lady invites one to her body and mindset,
it's fitting to show respect, old-fashioned etiquette,
whether she be the French queen Marie-Antoinette
or an upcoming soprano from the outskirts of Toledo.
I've learnt that men are not the only ones with ego.

2 *A Delicious Spasm*

What's the point an old man recounting his memoirs,
if he fails to mention any going-ons in boudoirs?
When I was eleven, on the threshold of puberty,
I met this girl (whom I shall discreetly describe as B).
Four years my senior, she was in fact the sister
of the tutor with whom I'd taken lodgings in Padua.
This B would be my first love, my *primera amorosa*.
A great reader of novels, she took me under her care.
Saying she had no time to wait until I was dressed,
she'd come every morning to my room to comb my hair,
wash my face, neck, often while I was still in bed,
mingling my daily ablutions with caresses of enthusiasm.
I was too shy, too innocent to reciprocate her actions,
which spurred this Venetian boy to a delicious spasm.

3 The Trees Are Moving

To this day one childhood memory wounds me.
I'm in a boat. From a low bed I see the tops of trees
which appear to be slipping away of their own will.
This sight, of course, arouses my astonishment.
'Look, dear mother! Look! The trees are moving.
Tell me, how is it that trees can walk by themselves?'
'It's the boat moving. Not the trees. Get dressed!'
she replied. But this phenomenon wouldn't let me rest.
Is it possible, I wonder, that the Sun stays still
and it is in fact us humans who rotate from East to West?
That's when my mother scolds me for my silliness.
Now, though the memory hurts, my early questioning
marked my toddling step towards philosophy's wing.

4 Scandalous Pranks

In youthful Venice we played many scandalous pranks
such as untying gondolas from their moorings.
We'd be killing ourselves laughing from the banks
of the Grand Canal as we watched the liberated gondolas
drift this way, drift that way – a flotilla of disorder!
We'd delight in the curses the gondoliers hurled at us
when they witnessed their gondolas doing a runner.
But the prank we always found the most hilarious
was to suddenly rouse a midwife out of her slumber:
'Hurry, someone's in labour at such and such address!'
By the time the poor midwife showed up, all breathless,
we'd be in stitches, imagining the reaction she'd get
from some none-too-pleased doddering mum-to-be.
'Be off! Me pregnant? At my age! Eighty-three!'

5 *That Addictive Flutter*

I did play with following the ecclesiastic path.
Alas! I wasn't cut out to be a man of the cloth.
For a time I dared to pursue a military career
but watching innocent lives go to collateral waste
was not what the Good Lord had ordained for me.
For a while, a librarian, shepherding flocks of books
suited me fine though on gambling I'd been hooked.
So I gambled on love's self-evolving wheel of fortune.
Yes, even when the chips were down, I dearly hoped
the dice of romance would roll towards my door.
Long may the Queen of Hearts lean her lady-bloom
over the slope of Casanova's love-smitten shoulder.
Anything for the sake of that addictive flutter.
Oh let me be a lamb led to chubby Cupid's altar.

6 *By Misconception Damned*

Before I get around to divulging my Soho trysts
I daresay a taste of my chequered bio won't go amiss.
April 1725 chose to deliver me to the sign of Aries,
thus making me astrological offspring of the Ram
whose horns, I'd have you know, point to brain faculties.
Nevertheless, I have been by misconception damned
to fit the mould of wham-bam-thank-you-mam.
So with no false modesty – that overrated virtue –
allow me to pay myself my own unsung due.
Despite my many a dalliance of the amorous kind,
I like to think of myself as philosophically inclined.
And endowed, as I was, with an enormous IQ,
I set about (with respect) rewriting Homer's *Iliad*,
though the original, I have to say, was not bad.

7 *Geared Up to Recite*

Good people, you've heard not even half my tale.
Who knows what other endowments may prevail?
Just give me a glass of the finest Venetian vino,
and I'm all geared up to recite Dante, Ariosto.
Ask me nicely, and I'll burst into bits of bel canto.
By eighteen I was busy impressing Pope Benedict
that I wasn't cut out to be your average Catholic.
All well and good confessing and mouthing the rosary,
but the soul thrives better in the soil of poetry.
For what is poetry if not the tree that bears its own
word–music from the acoustic roots of the throat?
But who am I to talk of poetic do's and don'ts?
Many speak their rhyming hearts into a microphone,
but for me poetry is best declaimed from a pillow.

8 *Frisked by Dover Security*

I'll skip over my escape from a Venetian prison
and cut to my mid-June arrival in London.
Since the English weather was known for its vagary,
only the optimistic, the ill-informed or the foolhardy
would choose November or December when the winter
winds gather the best of their gale-force fury.
I nonetheless exercised a measure of common sense
by arming my person with a sensible umbrella.
It must be this appendage (the natives call a brollie)
that causes the English to move at a reserved trot,
feeling themselves too superior to move at a gallop.
But my confession to being French by naturalisation
prompted Dover Security to frisk me top to bottom –
which, I must say, was a not unpleasant sensation.

9 *Effnic Or Ethnic?*

After Immigration had granted me the right-of-way,
followed by a polite nod and Sir, have a pleasant stay,
I half-expected the skies to roll out their grey carpet,
but summer's shimmering blue greeted my first step
towards the fashionable district known as Pall Mall
where a three-storeyed house awaited my arrival.
By then travel-lagged, I was gasping for a cup of tea
(for which the English tastebud is legendary).
This beverage my hostess provided without much ado,
informing me that it was called a cuppa or a brew.
But however hard I tried to get my famished tongue
around the labyrinth of the Oxford lexicon,
my Venetian accent was assumed to be foreign or thick.
Once I overheard what sounded like effnic or ethnic?

10 *Soho Here I Come*

Crossing from Calais to Dover would cost me six guineas
but I was curious about the English and their liberties.
Indeed, I felt a tremor all the way down to my knees,
just thinking of the district known locally as Soho –
a name (I later learnt) rooted in the hunting cry
Sohooo! that would herald a stag's death-throes
as royals cheered to see the hounded creature laid low –
its final grimace destined for above the mantelpiece.
Mind you, to be fair, I'm talking of Soho 1763,
when stag-bashing for silver-spooned land-led gentry
was a civilised entertainment beyond the commoner.
But I'd rather lose myself in the theatre's wonder
or be conversing one-to-one in a seedy tavern,
happily watching the candle of my heart burn.

11 *Neither Troll Nor Trollop*

At the risk, dear friends, of appearing to digress,
I must say that I was very much impressed
by the quaintness of some street names of London –
a testament to the waywardness of the English tongue
as well as to that nation's eccentric imagination.
Signs pointing me towards Butts Lane, Petticoat Lane,
Hookers Mews, not to mention Bollocks Avenue,
left this foreigner disoriented as well as amused.
Pausing at the crossroads, I did my best to desist
from peregrinating along such beckoning byways,
however suggestive of hidden wanton promise.
Needless to say, I, Casanova, could little resist
the sound of Trollop Road where, on my brief stop,
I encountered alas neither troll nor trollop.

12 *Winchester Geese*

Trust the English for reaping the best of both worlds,
when it comes to discreetly nuanced usage of words.
No foreigner would dream of saying 'Surreyside Stews'
when referring to those quickly-snatched brothel screws.
One wintry evening I was only too pleased to discover
what amorous delights can be paid for undercover.
For the Romans geese were used for a burglar alarm,
but the visitor, new to London, will be most charmed
to learn ladies of the night are entitled Winchester Geese,
who for an agreed fee will grant the famished some release.
I have many a time and oft been goosed (I hasten to admit)
by such unfeathered geese, it could be called a habit.
Thanks to the Bishop of Winchester (my hostess tell me)
for adding brothel earnings to his well-blessed treasury.

13 *Meat and Two Veg*

Why the mention of meat and two veg should bring
restrained giggles to a posh private gathering,
I could not help but find odd, if not bewildering,
being a newcomer to the ways of English nuance
as much as to their pomp, damp and circumstance.
Then, at a soiree, my tactful hostess, a fashionable
baroness familiar with the most exotic of edibles,
took me out of my forgivably foreign ignorance
when she confided meat and two veg meant testicles.
Thereupon I thanked her and expressed my admiration
for the English mastery of verbal manipulation
that dares to conjure up such delightful idioms.
How can one argue with a metaphor so aptly culinary?
Pleasing both to the carnivore and to the veggie.

14 *Periodic Nose-bleeds*

Having endured periodic nose-bleeds as a child,
I can well empathise with the monthly-magic-tide
that binds a woman to the ways of the moon.
Though prone to the most sudden of mood-swings,
I make no such lunar claims for my nasal bleedings.
My grandma, dear nonna, had taken me under her wing
(my mother, having buggered off, as the English put it,
to strut the London stage and dream of rave reviews).
To cure my nose-bleeds, grandma took me to see a witch.
Not the panto kind wielding the sceptre of a broomstick,
but one steeped in tarot cards and nature's brews.
She locked me in a chest that still feels like a black box.
But that black box did the trick. My nose-bleeds stopped.

15 *All My Mama's Fault*

There are times, you know, when I'm a bit depressed,
or let's say when I'm feeling not at my friskiest,
I'd wonder whether, had my mother been a more
affectionate type, more cuddly, more touchy-feely,
I would have grown up to love (no, make that adore)
the female sex with such an unbridled frenzy.
One day some psychologist will come up with the key
to fly the lock to Casanova's subconscious door.
But I'm not the kind to lie on a shrink's couch.
No, I'd rather be laid back unattired. Slouched
between some daintily embroidered linen sheet,
laying bare my vulnerable self at a stranger's feet.
Oh my mother surely has a lot to answer for.
It's all my mama's fault I'm this love-scarred lover.

16 *The Cell in Celibate*

How can I, a well brought-up Christian, ever comply
with God's instruction to go forth and multiply,
if I were to cage myself within monastic walls?
Who am I, mere mortal, this holy flesh to deny,
when the Good Lord has granted me a pair of balls
(to which the English give the odd name bollocks).
The heart's tick is shadowed by the tick of clocks
and numbered are our days. Soon the grim reaper calls.
So there and then I said farewell to my cassock.
Put off by the subliminal cell in that word celibate,
I returned to Padua to complete my doctorate
in law. But can you imagine yours truly in wig and gown?
No thanks. Sweet love would overrule all legal ambition,
once Venus had mounted this willing Venetian.

17 *Love-rat*

Though my other name be Jacques, I'll tell you flat,
I'm no Jack-the-lad. And certainly no love-rat.
To use that term for a cheat of two-timing intent,
is to insult the rat, that humbly squeaking rodent
that served as steed for the Hindu god, Ganesha,
that drew the carriage of transformed Cinderella,
that creature who forewarns of a sinking ship
in order for passengers to cower towards safety.
To the modern ear, love-rat may sound hip.
There are those who embrace it wholeheartedly –
a laddish title. Manhood's medal. Another notch.
Yet, strange, how some ladies are drawn to such.
I accept that rats are not exactly monogamous,
but that comes from an overactive hypothalamus.

18 *Grey Thames Grey Seine*

The River Thames is as grey as the River Seine.
But that, I have to say, is where the similarity ends.
For most, the Seine evokes Parisian romance.
But for me, that river conjures up turbulence
when Revolution reared its guillotine head
and the headless bore witness to monarchy's
disrupted divinity. For a Royalist such as myself,
the word that comes to mind is mindless anarchy.
In the heart of Paris stood heaving voyeur crowds
when Damien's flesh was damned to public spectacle
for his bungled attempt to shed King Louis' blood.
Even fancy crinolined ladies clamoured to ogle
as four horses severed a man from his own torso.
To my shame, I chose to hire a narrow discreet window.

19 *At My Wits' End*

Strange, but however insufferable my heart's pain,
I could not bear to end it all in the river Seine.
Yet, for some reason I'm still to discover,
on one typically debilitating winter evening,
I played with the idea of climbing London Tower
and throwing my wretched self to the Thames.
Doing myself in (as is said in the vernacular).
I wouldn't blame my mood solely on the weather.
There was something I couldn't put my finger on.
That candid Monsieur Voltaire, penniless in England,
describes the English as a nation of philosophers.
I know they value understatement as much as freedom.
But having been rejected by a young prostitute,
I was at my wits' end. And that's the God's truth.

20 *Dumped*

The word 'dump' always brings a throat to my lump.
(So sorry, English isn't my mother tongue.)
But given the choice, I'd rather be dumped than dump.
For me, breaking another's heart is unthinkable.
I'd rather the lady lay her cards on the table,
even if that means harsh words hurled in my ear.
Though rejection wounds to the core, why squabble?
Let her tell me to go to hell. Tell me to disappear.
I pay heed and follow such instructions to the letter.
But first I spill my heart out before taking my exit.
Let her know that I'm (as the English say) gutted.
That I'm her marionette. That I'm her willing dupe.
Using modern parlance, I say, 'Keep me in the loop!
Please let's stay tender friends till the day we droop.'

21 *The Colour of Incognito*

What does it mean, to live life to the very full,
if not living life in the manner of a carnival.
Faced with the pole-faced custodians of taboo,
a dose of carnival may yet come to your rescue.
Yes, prancing in a mask to defeat the frowns,
boring old farts (excuse my French) become clowns,
macho gallants show up in sequin-spangled gowns.
Poised on the tightrope between to sin or not to sin,
I find it always helps to step out of my skin
into the guise of anonymously motley Harlequin.
Role-play for me means just that. Rolling as you play
according to the misrules of commedia dell'arte.
Behind a mask prejudice goes out of the window.
For who can truly decipher the colour of incognito?

22 *Both He and She*

It was in 1744, when I was merely sweet nineteen,
that I met someone who, genderwise, was inbetween,
though I hesitate to resort to the hyphenated
to describe the angelic Angiola Calori, a celebrated
diva whose ambivalence embraced both he and she.
It never failed to beguile how with flamboyant ease
shy Angiola would metamorphose into the manly Bellino
who'd make swooning women forget he was a castrato.
But I discovered with my own two gobsmacked eyes
that Bellino was in fact a woman in castrato guise.
Yes, this soprano of ravishing three-octave highs,
with the little help of a fake penis for accomplice,
would brandish male and female below the midriff.
I thought such double bliss must be hard to resist.

23 *When the Holy Sanctifies the Mouth*

Consider yourselves lucky you lovers whose senses,
having been satiated, and thereby requiring rest,
can fall back on the intellectual ravishments
afforded by the mind. After much vigorous dalliance,
how lovely to lie back and exchange introspections
of the mind, while basking in love's copious secretions.
Sweet words in the ear can awaken the nether sections.
Long may lovers mingle sighs with poetry's paradox,
their listening blood deaf to percentages and stocks.
I'm not suggesting that in post-coitally unwinding
you should turn your tongues to academic analysing
bounded by binaries and bone-dry post-modernising.
No, I'm thinking more along the lines of the luminary.
When pillow talk sanctifies the mouth, no talk is dirty.

24 *In the Arms of the Enlightenment*

Philosophy has never once done me any harm.
In fact, all my life I've never been more charmed
than by the union of the senses (all five) and the mind.
Must we celebrate the cranium and ignore the spine?
The sheer joy of debating paradoxical Spinoza
brought me both physically and spiritually closer
to argumentative Leonilda, whom I'd met in St Petersburg.
There we feasted on each other and Pushkin's noble words.
As for shy Clementina, after a bout of mutual consent,
we'd argue tit for tat the fine points of the Enlightenment.
Yes, we shared many a ding-dong metaphysical chinwag
after a course of what the English would label a shag.
Oh those pre-dawn cuddles along the Piazza San Marco,
our breathing punctuated by the pigeons and Plato!

That enchanting Murano nun still consumes my memory.
(Better not say her name lest I be chastised by the Pope.)
Though wedded to Christ, vowed to chastity and poverty,
she was open to the persuasion of frail flesh and bone.
Well-read in the *Confessions* of Saint Augustine,
this nun would often refer to herself as a libertine.
An aura of purity oozed from her every cloistered pore
(though purity is not all it has been cracked up to be).
Sleeping with a nun is not exactly a habit of mine
(pardon the pun intended) but my God! How divine
to behold her disrobed. She never failed to enchant me
when she unveiled her limbs in favour of the scanty.
O sweetest of nuns, still winsome at the age of eighty-one,
my sincere thanks for both your ablution and absolution.

26 *Lay Clothing*

Once my quick-witted nun suggested a rendezvous
beside our Republic's fighting hero – Colleoni's statue.
So, at the agreed time of sunset, there was I
nervously pacing the piazza under that Titan-eyed
figure of the past now perched on a horse of bronze.
The thought of my sweet nun and I being observed
by a dead equestrian gave my desire an extra edge.
All of a sudden, out of the shadows there emerged
a man masked in the glitter of a spangled balaclava.
The fellow approached me in so menacing a manner
that I was sorry not to have brought along my pistols.
But the masked one then offered me a peaceful hand
which turned out to be that of my disguised darling –
even more angelic in what she called her lay clothing.

27 *Inclined to the Savoury*

To foreign dishes there are those who say no thank you.
Not me. With bookworm eye I enjoy perusing the menu
for an unfamiliar titbit that might well titillate the palate.
Why let a pre-conditioned mindset colonise your plate
by dividing and ruling the borders of your tastebuds?
I recall partaking even of plain hot-buttered spuds
(the earthy common English expression for potato)
when a bit peckish I promenaded winter-deep Soho.
Of course, I am by nature more inclined to the savoury,
an Olla podrida or a Neapolitan macaroni, preferably
with glutinous codfish from pure Newfoundland waters.
(How long they'll stay unpolluted, that's another story.)
In the mansion of the mouth there is enough room
to welcome all shades of this blessing known as food.

28 *Exposing My Faulty Grammar*

How fondly I do recall a certain English courtesan
known through the length and breadth of courtly England.
The lady in question became an eminent feature of Soho.
Sadly, I lacked the confidence to speak her lingo.
My English, I'm ashamed to say, was not up to scratch,
though my aching back was longing to be scratched.
This good lady was more than my intellectual match.
I who had parodied Racine and translated Molière
was still to master the language of Shakespeare.
I suppose I might have made more of an impression,
had I dared serenade her in received pronunciation.
But for fear of exposing to her my faulty grammar,
I had to resort to the odd pantomimic gesture.
Helping brush up her Italian was my timid offer.

29 *A Romantic Rendezvous*

If in Venice you're stuck for a romantic rendezvous,
a gondola might sound like a predictable venue.
Sleeping on a mattress in a carriage along a ruined
road to Riga can release what Catholics call sin.
A cosy apartment at 32 Piazza di Spagna in Rome
has been known to trigger two strangers to disrobe.
And if you're hoping to roll with Baroness von Roll,
a rented castle in Switzerland would do nicely.
But why splash out on a princely pretentious folly
when you can do the business on that final plot
where all flesh bound for oblivion goes to rot?
Entwined with a widow on her husband's tombstone,
I felt the urge to weep for what my lips left untold
as if her hubbie's shortened days had been my own.

30 *A Black Roman?*

I couldn't help observing that the island known as England
has a different colour from that of the European continent.
Same way as the River Thames has a different flavour
from its Parisian counterpart – the Seine stirring up for me
cosy tête-a-têtes with Madame de Pompadour over coffee,
as opposed to polite tea-sipping with my English hostess,
who managed to find me a local French-speaking chef
as well as a black valet of impeccable bearing.
I must say I found his gesticulating curiously endearing.
His impression of a stiff-upper-lip-gent enchanted me.
We would often converse for he spoke Italian fluently.
He confided he'd traced a black Roman in his family tree.
When he declared his dream to play Caesar at Drury Lane,
my admiration for the fellow's ambition was unrestrained.

I'm amused the way the English unleash their brollies
in anticipation of overhead unpredictabilities.
Is this a tribal precaution? Or a pre-emptive strike
against the gathering cavalry of grey clouds?
Now I understand the expression on your bike.
For who wants to walk when it's raining cats and dogs
and God knows what other domesticated quadrupeds.
Enough to make a foreigner seek political asylum
in the warm harbour of some stranger's bed.
Grateful for a heaven-sent flesh-and-blood union.
Needless to say, such happiness has its setbacks,
for after one of many such encounters came the shock
of discovering I'd contracted a dose of the dreaded pox!
I demanded a second opinion, which would shock the doc!

32 *Pillow Talk*

In the interest of what's called political correctness,
I tremble to make mention of that Jewish Countess
who introduced me both to her midriff and her Midrash,
a sacred text she revealed with uninhibited panache.
Indeed, we became extremely tender physical friends.
This good lady was also of such a voracious mind
we'd discuss the nature of the atom as we reclined.
Never once was she backward in coming right forward –
a superb embodiment of Biblical flesh becoming Word.
I had such a job keeping up with her mental stamina
that I unashamedly decided to plunder the Kabbala
for mystic soundbites to intrigue her grey matter.
Oh to hear her breathe out pillow-talk in Hebrew
made my gentile mouth pay her deserving due.

33 *Muse in Tutu*

Aptly named Sextus Propertius coupled in Latin couplets
with a courtesan (in elegiac couplets I hasten to add).
In twinned rhymes he preserves his singular Cynthia
whose eyes could ensnare like the arrows of Scythia.
Whoever be this Cynthia, this flesh-and-blood Muse,
I say good on her, for I can think of nothing sweeter
than a learned courtesan inspiring poetic metre.
No disrespect to Apollo but I say let Venus prevail
in maintaining the Muse as subliminally female.
Even now I fondly think of that Russian courtesan
whose poise of neck rivalled that of a swan.
To the Muse of Ballet she said she had vowed herself.
After she'd rejected me for arabesques and pirouettes,
I grieved for days on end thinking of her tutu-less.

34 *Don't Be Shy*

I'm not so sure I should be telling you this,
for my revelation may prove somewhat embarassing
to ears that are prudish and easily offended.
But I'll keep it clean. Well, there am I, the guest
of a gaunt-featured rougely-complexioned Duchess.
Before long my hostess catches me off-guard.
Against my face she presses her bosom hard.
I don't know whether I should reciprocate or not.
Then she makes a beeline for my vulnerable spot,
saying: Don't be shy! Show a lady what you've got!
Not fully at ease with being ensnared in her trap,
I cry: 'Dear lady, heaven forbid! I'll give you the clap!'
It seemed ungracious of me to have refused her offer.
And I still feel a twinge of shame for so deceiving her.

35 *Hell-bound according to Pope Gregory*

Pope Gregory (later Saint) in his fortieth homily
(I am still to read his previous thirty-nine)
speaks harsh words against adornments that are costly.
Garments that glitter. Jewels of the bling-bling kind.
Such, the Pope argues, are trappings of vainglory.
In short, finery is the breeding ground for sin,
hence those garbed in razzle-dazzle designer linen
find themselves hell-bound for everlasting torment.
St Gregory warns against fashion's serpentine path
which leads the ostentatious directly to God's wrath.
But I must confess I am moved to introspection
when opulent Peking silk slithers to the ground.
And pity a Pope blind to the sight of diamonds
sweetly rolling like ice-cubes down a chaste bosom.

36 *In Folio*

Now, nearing the end, I recall my sojourn in Soho
where I'd purchased a few erotic prints in folio.
Not so much for the beauty of their execution,
but for the graphic nature of their love-positions.
I wasn't surprised to learn they were the oeuvre
of an Englishman who in muted greys had re-configured
the fundamentals of the Kama Sutra – an ancient text
where the Hindus charmingly describe coitus as congress.
Of course, the prints held me enchanted, intrigued,
though some postures portrayed were out of my league –
requiring at least the cobra-like spinal flexibility
of a Chinese acrobat somersaulting towards infinity.
Not wanting to do myself damage, I thought I'd miss
out on such strenuous shenanigans lest I slip a disc.

Senior citizens like myself may try an aphrodisiac,
which is much more poetic than prosaic Prozac,
for history reveals elderly Emperors, Sultans, Tsars,
who have relied on kawyar (the Persian for caviar,
meaning strong cake, as distinct from English cup cake).
Excavated oyster shells (none so far proven to be fake)
have convinced the most sceptical of Western scholars
that oysters were boosters to third-age Cro-Magnons.
My Arab friends point me to peppered milk of almonds
as a sure-fire way to rekindle passion's embers.
For Moctezuma it was chili chocolate by the tumblers.
But to restore an old love and ripen a young one,
as well as rouse whatever slumbers betwixt the knees,
I highly recommend Scotland's sea-salted cheese.

38 *Twilight Manoeuvring*

Does the weight of years immune us to passion's flame?
Is it farewell to fleshly frolics when a zimmer frame
becomes the vehicle of our twilight manoeuvring?
Tell me, don't the geriatric deserve one final fling?
Speaking these words, I find myself stuttering
as my life's highs and lows rewind before my eyes.
Thank God, blessed with memory, both long and short,
I haven't (fingers crossed) lost any of my marbles,
though marbles take me back to a traumatic childhood.
My unexpurgated memoirs provide me much comfort
while philosophy keeps me in tune with my ageing blood.
But between silver porcelain, evening frocks, Cretan wine,
I must thank life for showing me a glimpse of paradise.
Oh to be peered at once again through operatic eyes.

39 *Begin by Loving Yourself*

If you want to be loved, then simply love.
From experience likeness begets likeness.
If unloved, why not begin by loving yourself?
it's true your inward spark may be over-ignited
while hers stays unlit in her heart's fireplace.
That being the case, you'll be having a foretaste
of a love that goes by the name unrequited.
But no reason for you to retreat into your shell.
Heaven's goodies can come wrapped in hell.
So why fence yourself in self-pitying angst?
Learn to flow with the rise and fall of romance.
Ask yourself if your words are mere pretence.
Maybe your sweet whispered nothings are just that.
Not loving. But being, as the English say, a twat!

40 *Epilogue: A Blue Plaque?*

A shame Carlisle House where I had stayed in Soho
would be doomed to embers like that of Marco Polo.
Now replaced (according to the London Gazetteer)
by the pious bulk of St Patrick's Roman Catholic Church.
Those cassocked ones who put on pedestals the celibate
can only dream of what went on at parties called private.
Then London's high society politely queued up to get laid
in the anonymous arms of a Venetian masquerade.
Yet, if I'm honest, from time to time I regret the lack
of some manner of royally commissioned plaque.
A small posthumous memento to Casanova's sojourn.
But when it comes down to the matter of colour,
I wouldn't choose blue. No, I'd rather go for a red
plaque discreetly positioned over my Soho bed.